SpringerBriefs in Educational Communications and Technology

Series Editors
J. Michael Spector, University of North Texas, Denton, TX, USA
M.J. Bishop, University System of Maryland, Adelphi, MD, USA
Dirk Ifenthaler, University of Mannheim, Mannheim, Germany

More information about this series at http://www.springer.com/series/11821

Joseph Frantiska Jr.

Interface Development for Learning Environments

Establishing Connections Between Users and Learning

Springer

Joseph Frantiska Jr.
School of Education
Walden University
North Chelmsford, MA, USA

ISSN 2196-498X ISSN 2196-4998 (electronic)
SpringerBriefs in Educational Communications and Technology
ISBN 978-3-030-14481-4 ISBN 978-3-030-14482-1 (eBook)
https://doi.org/10.1007/978-3-030-14482-1

Library of Congress Control Number: 2019935817

This Springer imprint is published by the registered company Springer Nature Switzerland AG
The registered company address is: Gewerbestrasse 11, 6330 Cham, Switzerland

This brief is dedicated to my mother Madeline and to my late father Joseph Sr.

Preface

As technology has become more sophisticated, engineers have used various means to allow them to interact with systems that they have developed or use in order to develop other systems. As educational technology had matured, educators have also needed to wrestle with these same interfacing problems. In doing so, their students or other practitioners can interact with complex learning environments in an optimal fashion.

In Chap. 1, the background and tools of interface design are discussed along with an illustrative example used throughout the brief to provide a structured approach that is applicable to a wide variety of situations. Chapter 2 examines the theoretical background upon which the techniques and procedures are based on. Chapter 3 focuses on the techniques and procedures that form the basis for the development of interfaces. Storyboarding and prototyping are as applicable to the field of educational technology development as they are to the high-tech arena. Chapter 4 builds upon the preceding chapters by adding various design approaches that form the skeleton of an environment. The meat on the bones of this skeleton is the graphical component that is discussed in the remainder of Chap. 4. The subject of Chap. 5 further adds to the interface as static graphics provide limited interaction. It is here that animation, video, and sound are introduced to provide a much richer and more productive environment. Finally, while all of these components play an important role in modern learning environments and how they interact with systems and people, the written word is still of great importance. Chapter 6 discusses how text can quickly but succinctly put forth ideas and instruction.

It is the goal of this brief to aid the educator in developing interfaces between people and online learning environments. In this way, they can create learning environments that will interact with their students. The students can efficiently interact with the learning environment, which will then allow them to maximize their interaction with the world in general.

Background and Significance

The Merriam-Webster dictionary defines an interface as "the place at which independent and often unrelated systems meet and act on or communicate with each other." In the case of humans interfacing with computer systems, interfaces have become more and more complex. This can be both good and bad with the good being derived from the vast information that can be represented to the user. The bad aspect is that the instructional designer must be cognizant of both the information available and how to present it to the user. This two-pronged approach ensures that both ends of the human-computer interface are considered. The interface acts as a bridge between the human and machine and needs to act as a translator between the two. The signals generated by the machine are radically different from the images and text that the human understands. Not only is the interface required to select the necessary information but to display it in formats that are optimally useful and intelligible.

The designer needs to assess the information available and not only how to present it to the user insofar as the efficient usage of screen area but also with respect to the user's inherent learning style and abilities. In order to do this, a structured approach that properly addresses both aspects is needed. This brief aims to fill this need.

North Chelmsford, MA, USA Joseph Frantiska Jr.

Contents

Chapter 1
Interface Basics

An Illustrative Example

In order to fully examine all aspects of interface development features within this brief, an illustrative example will be progressively developed with each chapter's content building upon that of those that precede it. The illustrative example that will be used is the construction of a website/learning object that teaches about how to tie various knots. While they are of particular interest to the sailing community, they can also demonstrate how forces work together in a physics class. Also, there is an analogy between physical knots and the mathematical field of knot theory. Finally, outside of the classroom, it can be of interest to specific groups such as scouting and sailing classes (adults and children).

User Interface Design

An interface is comprised of two entities: a set of media dictated by the required functionality of the environment and the arrangement (the "look and feel") of these media to be as effective as possible. It is the job of the instructional designer to understand and decide how that arrangement is perceived and experienced by the user in an instructional product (Jones & Farquhar, 1997; McClelland, Eisman, & Stone, 2000). The design of the interface should be as helpful to the user as possible; its components should assist the user in facilitating their work through ease of use, ease of access, and optimal utility (Khan, 1997; McClelland et al., 2000). The instrument panel of a car or aircraft is an interface. Its purpose is to allow the operator to control the vehicle as required. For this to happen, the controls, displays, and indicators on the panel must provide the proper type and amount of information for the safe and efficient operation of the vehicle. In addition to the

J. Frantiska Jr., *Interface Development for Learning Environments*,
SpringerBriefs in Educational Communications and Technology,
https://doi.org/10.1007/978-3-030-14482-1_1

inherent functionality of the controls and indicators, their placement is equally imperative; what good is an accurate, readable fuel gauge if it's located in a hard to see place?

In comparing a user interface to an instrument panel, what was used was an analogy; a comparison between two things based upon similarities of like features. For example, calling a computer an "electronic brain." When creating an interface, the designer must decide whether to use a visual analogy or a metaphor. Visual analogies describe something that is unknown by comparing it with something known (Dove, 2011). In the knot tying learning environment, an example of a visual analogy might be showing the learner an animation of DNA and its double helix shape. This helps the learner visualize the mechanics of a knot. One problem with such a visual analogy is that the learner might infer that the rope or line used in knot tying interacts in the same way as do the strands of DNA; this is not correct.

A metaphor is a type of analogy in the form of a term or phrase that is applied to something to which it is not literally applicable to suggest a resemblance (Davidson-Shivers & Rasmussen, 2018). An instructional metaphor is a representation of a mental model that helps to guide learners through a learning experience (Driscoll, 2005; Lohr, 2003). An example of an instructional metaphor for teaching proper arm movement for chest compressions in cardiopulmonary resuscitation is to have the learner envision their arms as the piston within a cylinder of an engine. The piston moves straight up and down, the most efficient way to accomplish the task. For a visual analogy or a metaphor to be useful it must be something familiar to the learner and should complement the content or the idea being presented in the environment. Analogies and metaphors are often used in computer-based training and learning environments to help learners understand a specific feature of the instruction. According to Nielsen (2000), metaphors are useful for providing a unifying framework for individual pages within their associated website. Creating a history website that was developed as a "museum" uses the museum as a metaphor to create a unifying framework. Otherwise, the site could have been nothing more than disparate pages of history information. The museum gave the site a structure in that each type of history (technological, political, etc.) was viewed as a linear progression through time. Also, by setting up the connecting hallways, learners could see that at various points in time, different types of history can impact each other.

Human–computer interaction (HCI) is the study of the relations between humans and computers. It contains as a subfield, the design of user or human–computer interfaces (Saxena, Kothari, Jain, & Khurana, 2002).

The creation of the field of HCI unified the pertinent parts of the areas of computer science, psychology, linguistics, sociology, and human factors. The HCI design process creates interactive computer systems so they allow people to accomplish their tasks in an efficient manner. To accomplish this, the design must be user-friendly. That is, the interface is understandable with appropriate controls that are accessible and readable. An example of a poor user interface design would be if something goes wrong with the system and there either is no error message or a message that does not accurately address the problem. This can frustrate the learner and most importantly interferes with the alleviation of the problem and the continuance of the learner's task. Interface design is related to the software engineering part of computer science. HCI research covers a wide range of topics from the effect of the interface on people to the techniques, methods, and tools that designers use to build interactive systems. Hence, the foundation issues are:

1. Understand the needs and desires of the target audience.
2. Given the appropriate target audience, scrutinize what the learners do with computer systems and their interfaces based on the learner's tasks and requirements.
3. Once the audience and tasks are determined, identify how the interface should function, how it should respond to the learner, and its appearance.
4. Develop tools to help designers build better interfaces.
5. Evaluating the properties of human–computer interfaces and their effect on people to ensure good quality.

Another discipline under the umbrella of HCI is human factors or ergonomics which is a subfield of applied psychology. Its purpose is to improve the design of machines so that people can use them efficiently; make the device accommodate the user and not the other way around. While ergonomics has been also applied to everything from the proper design of furniture to the optimal dimensions of a computer monitor, it can also be used to determine the best possible aspects of a human–computer interface.

Cognitive psychology is concerned with psychological processes such as memory, reasoning, problem-solving, and perception. HCI employs cognitive psychology for models and theories of human–computer interaction. While human factors techniques are used to ensure that people are comfortable interacting with their interface and can utilize it to the optimal extent, the same must be provided for a user's cognitive abilities and restrictions. Know the audience! What are the ages of the learners? What is their level of prior knowledge of the subject matter? An interface that is confusing and cluttered to a 6 year old may be fine for someone in middle school. Conversely, an interface constructed with the 6 year old in mind can be frustrating to the middle school student who sees it as lacking the components necessary for the interface to be efficient. We must be cognizant of the capabilities and associated limitations of high- and low-knowledge learners.

Aircraft cockpit design was one of the first usages of research into the design of computer–human interfaces. World War 2 saw the then new field of human factors applied to optimize the design of cockpits to give pilots maximum efficiency and usage of the instruments and controls. Can the pilot reach the controls? Does the seat height need to be changed? Will he be able to read the instruments in low light conditions? The current field of computer interface design has its roots in this research. Donald Norman, one of the leading researchers in this field, suggested seven principles of good design applicable to all human-centered development (Norman, 1998):

1. Begin with a user needs assessment of user needs. This includes watching users in the process of performing the task that the new product is intended to aid. Observe and learn so that the solution will fit the problem.
2. What other similar products (solutions) exist? Can they be applied to the problem? Some of their features?
3. From the outputs of items 1 and 2, develop a description of the users' needs. Each need should be validated by observations and data.
4. As a direct result of item 3, develop some prototypes with some of the methodologies and tools previously discussed. Review them with the users and get their reactions. Modify the prototypes with their feedback.
5. With the final prototype and description of user needs, write an operations manual if one is needed. It should be as concise and informative as possible.
6. Begin the design process working with the manual and the prototypes.
7. Test and revise as needed.

In the early days of human–computer interaction, the first method available for users to interact with computers was through a command language interface. This involved the tedious, time consuming process of typing in commands to a computer terminal. Unlike today's "point and click" graphical interface where a learner starts an application by double-clicking on its icon, starting up that application with a command language interface may require numerous commands typed in from memory (no online help facility). Direct manipulation systems are today's graphic user interface (GUI) now seen as an industry standard for with everything from automated teller machines to air traffic control systems. Shneiderman et al. (2016) argued that the usefulness of GUIs arose from their visual nature allowing the learner to see the objects instead of having to mentally visualize the tasks into the necessary commands as with command language systems. Each action produces a result in the task domain that is visible in the interface. Shneiderman related the basic principle to stimulus–response compatibility from the human factors realm. He claimed that the difficulty with text commands necessitated an appropriate representation or model of reality so that user interactions were more intuitive (Shneiderman et al., 2016).

Hypertext

Hypertext has long been a part of human–computer interaction as it imitates the way the brain works. Repeatedly, it is argued that hypertext may be critical in the advancement of nonlinear thinking (McKnight, Dillon, & Richardson, 1991). However, one of the main problems with hypertext is that it can cause severe difficulty with navigation for users if not designed properly (McKnight et al., 1991; Osgood, 1994). Hypertext indexing methods were found to often be inadequate and not necessarily focused on what the user needs to follow (McKnight et al., 1991).

As always, a good design based upon an understanding of the needs of the user and the problem at hand is the key to a complete, long-term solution (Berg, 2000).

McKnight et al. (1991) argue that there really is not much difference between hypertext and print reading. They point out that reading is not a thoroughly linear process, especially with experienced readers who rarely read a document in a strictly linear fashion from beginning to end. They may take many detours through the document in their journey from the beginning to the end. While hypertext represents a change in the presentation of text, it may not alter the way in which words are read by a reader.

Why are hypertext-based computer-aided learning systems called learning systems instead of teaching systems? Because their primary purpose is to teach a variety of subject matters to various learner audiences. Nevertheless, they do represent a theory of or at least an approach to instruction. They provide an environment in which exploratory or discovery learning may flourish. What distinguishes the appearance of a hypertext learning system from that of any other structured browsing and retrieval system is that the former usually provides a range of tools that considerably extend the basic navigation facilities.

Beeman et al. (1987) suggest that by requiring learners to move toward nonlinear thinking, they may also stimulate processes of integration and contextualization in a way not achievable by linear presentation techniques. He describes the most extensive attempt to develop hypertext in this direction as Brown University's Intermedia project. When learners simply follow the links offered in a passive way there is little reason to suppose that learning is any more effective than that from an old-fashioned branching program in the programmed instruction tradition. Intermedia seems to have demonstrated that a rich and extensive use of hypertext, with a carefully designed interface for the author as well as for the learner, can provide a successful environment for various kinds of learning activities.

An interpretation of the evaluations might be that such a system promotes effective learning only when the users are engaged in actively making their own connections and integrations at the conceptual level. Thirty years ago, the authors of programmed texts probably benefited in a similar way from engaging their subject matter at the level of detailed structure. There is no evidence here that simply navigating around the fixed links in Intermedia provides effective learning.

Perhaps the system that best exemplifies this class of computer-aided learning systems based on the provision of specific guidance tools built on top of a hypertext network is the HitchHiker's Guide. The principle espoused here is that of extending and tailoring basic hypertext facilities, not only with the standard aids to access, such as browsers, but also with tools that help the user to explore the material conceptually, such as guided tours, indexes, and quizzes.

The success of this system may also be due in no small measure to the care that has gone into the design of the interface. The learner is offered the consistent metaphor of a travel holiday to guide the exploration of the underlying instructional material.

Animation

Animation is another aspect of HCI that can be a mixture of promise and disappointment. It can provide a large amount of information within a concise presentation; one picture is worth a thousand words. Further, with so many pictures presented to the user in an animation, the user can be provided with not only information of a static process but also of dynamic processes that can be of a highly intricate nature. Animation is not used as much as it could be in human–computer interactions. Many in the literature argue that it can be very effective in establishing temper, in increasing sense of user identification, for influence, and for clarification. Baecker and Small (1995) describe many specific uses for animation including reviewing, showing the user where there are transitions in a process, to provide clear explanations of complex processes, show history of navigation patterns, and to provide user guidance.

However, there are skeptics about the usefulness of animations in user interfaces. Zhu and Grabowski (2006) conducted a study in which they found dubious results as the true effectiveness of animations versus static images. They stated their purpose as:

> …by investigating the instructional effects of two specific web-based animation strategies in facilitating participants' academic achievement: animated attention-gaining and animated elaboration strategies and compare them against static graphics. Animated arrows that directed learners' attention to specific image parts were used as an attention-gaining strategy to arouse participants' interest and aid them in attending to relevant cues and details. Animated text prompts were used as an elaboration strategy to provide additional information and emphasize the most important information in a corresponding instructional text passage.

They felt that based upon the existing literature, animations could be helpful in several ways. They hypothesized that animations with their dynamic nature would "be more likely to be dually coded 'deeper' and 'harder' into the long-term memory than are static graphics" with respect to Paivio's dual-coding theory. Focused on a cardiology example that "the animated attention-gaining strategy facilitated associative processing by highlighting specific parts of the heart using animated arrows. Animated elaboration strategies enabled referential processing by emphasizing the most important information in a corresponding text using animated text prompts." Thus, the animation seemed to help in the associative and referential processing where associative processing promotes connectivity with the verbal or visual system, while referential processing promotes connectivity between external stimuli and the verbal or visual system.

The subjects were placed in either a static images control group or an animation group. Another key aspect of these subjects was their degree of prior knowledge of the subject matter (heart anatomy and function). The authors cited the work of Mayer and Anderson (1992) in which learners with low prior knowledge achieved more learning when verbal and visual information were presented simultaneously. It was suggested that high prior knowledge learners could be able to construct referential connections between verbal and visual information and their existing knowledge on their own.

However, Zhu and Grabowski (2006) found that difference in achievement for the two subject groups was not significant; learners in the static graphics group performed equally well to those in the animation group. Additionally, their results showed that the lower prior knowledge learners performed equally well to those with high prior knowledge in all treatments. On the contrary, previous research showed that high prior knowledge learners performed better than learners with low prior knowledge regardless of the treatment. The authors believe this can be explained using dual-coding theory in that as previously mentioned, learners with low prior knowledge receive greater assistance when verbal and visual information is presented simultaneously (Mayer & Anderson, 1992). Animations need to be used appropriately when such a media form is needed to analyze and enhance highly dynamic processes.

Many of the principles in HCI are readily applicable to hypermedia-based learning environments. By the very fact that these environments act as a means of communications between humans and computers, human factors and usability need to be an integral part of learning environment design. Specifically, Shneiderman et al. (2016) point out the eight following principles of good interface design, his "Eight Golden Rules of User Interface Design":

1. *Consistency*—Consistency needs to be imposed in an environment to provide users with a standardized means of using the system. The same actions should be used in similar situations and the same terminology should be used in the environment's appearance, e.g., icons, menus, online help, etc. The environment needs to have a consistent appearance and means of operation (Nakaska & VanDusen, 2017).
2. *Allow learners with experience with the learning environment to use shortcuts*—The more familiar that a learner becomes with a site, the more they want to move to familiar parts quickly with a minimum amount of time working with the interface. This can be seen in the usage of any browser software whose users become increasingly familiar with various Internet sites; they want to set up these sites on the browser's "Favorites" pull-down menu.
3. *Offer informative feedback*—Feedback is the means of communications between a user and the computer via the interface. As the user performs an action and sends a request to the computer through the interface, an appropriate response from the interface needs to be sent. For minor actions, the response can be modest, while for major actions especially those requiring an error message, the response needs to be more significant.
4. *Design dialog to yield closure*—Sequences of actions should be organized into just that, a sequence; a logically ordered set of elements. Therefore, a sequence must possess a beginning, middle, and end. At the completion of a group of actions, feedback gives the operators the satisfaction of accomplishment/completion and an indication to prepare for the next group of actions (Zhu, Bonk, & Sari, 2017).

5. *Provide simple error handling*—Whenever possible, devise the system so that a serious error cannot be made. For example, when performing division, the quotient is divided by the divisor (e.g., 8/3, where 8 is the quotient and 3 is the divisor). In this situation don't allow the divisor to be zero as an undefined result will occur. If an error occurs, the system should offer simple, comprehensible methods for handling the error such as a warning message.
6. *Permit easy reversal of actions*—To avoid getting lost in the system or if an action fails, a user needs to be able to "back out" of a situation in a straightforward manner. The means of reversibility could be a single action, a data entry, or a small sequence of actions.
7. *Support internal locus of control*—Design the system to make users, especially the experienced ones, actors within the environment instead of reactors. Coupled with the informative feedback and simple error handling, users will have a sense of how they are progressing through the environment.
8. *Reduce short-term memory load*—Short-term memory within the human information-processing system is limited. Therefore, to avoid cognitive overload, displays need to be kept simple but not necessarily plain, multiple page displays should be concise with as few pages to accomplish the functionality as possible, and sufficient training time be allotted for codes, mnemonics, and sequences of actions.

Some practitioners argue that computer environments are useful in giving learners a rich learning experience by the very fact that there is a host of multimedia. Shneiderman (1993) asserts similarly that constructivist learning ideas are well-suited to hypermedia-based learning environment. He maintains that conventional, i.e., "old media," education is passive in nature, and that computers create an atmosphere for learner engagement. Shneiderman (1993) claimed that constructivism approach of computer-based learning differs from the computer-assisted instruction, intelligent computer instruction, and intelligent tutoring systems. The constructivist view spotlights interactive and discovery learning.

Assessment

Understand the Audience

Learners have certain characteristics related to instruction. For instance, they have the capability to hear oral communications and to read the printed word. These common qualities vary from one learner to another. For example, one may be able to read pages of printed text faster than another. Regardless of the degree of ability, instructional design is concerned with those qualities that affect the entire information-processing sequence of learning. These qualities may relate to sensory input, to internal processing, storage, and recovery of information, and finally to the organization of learner responses.

For such learner characteristics that are genetically determined, instructional design cannot employ learning as a means of altering these qualities. In these situations, instruction needs to be designed so that it does not overwhelm the cognitive capacities of the person in question. For instance, when a child is in the early stages of learning mathematics, some tasks may exceed their working memory.

Other learner qualities may affect learning at junctures of information processing that are more critical to instructional planning. There is a proposition that there may be innate capacity limits of the working memory where material is taken in and processed for memory storage. As previously discussed, the number of items that can be retained in memory simultaneously is shown by the immediate memory span of seven plus or minus two. The speed that learned concepts can be retrieved and identified may be measured by requiring individuals to respond as quickly as possible to specify whether pairs of letters match when the letters are physically different *(as F, f* or *E, e).* Due to this difference, the letters must be retrieved as concepts to be matched (Hunt, 1978). The speed and efficiency of this process is another individual quality that may be innately determined.

Some human qualities related to learning are inherently established. For instance, auditory acuity, although it may be aided by artificial amplification, is a fundamental property of a person's sensory system that is "built in" and that cannot be changed by learning. This category of qualities needs to be considered in instruction, such as the avoidance of low volume or poor quality recordings or streams (Gagne, Briggs, & Wager, 1992; Gagne, Wager, Golas, & Keller, 2005).

Define the Inputs

Once the learning objectives (what), information domain (where), and audience (who) are determined, the inputs that will be sent from a domain to an audience and governed by the learning objectives can be defined. The determination of inputs involves identifying the needs of the audience, the instructional content, instructional goals and objectives, teaching methods, evaluation materials, and instructional media. After the goals and objectives have been determined, and instructional activities and assessment techniques have planned, implementation of the planned instruction can begin with the students (Isman, 2005).

Define What Processing Occurs

Once the inputs are defined, the processing that they will be subjected to needs to be determined. This step is comprised of what the learner will be doing within the site. Therefore, the designer can be involved in a myriad of tasks such as creation of pages within the site concerning various types of media and instructional activities, connecting in the required manner to give a desired outcome. It is here that the development of testing to look for an acceptable level of domain knowledge takes place. The main goal of this step is to find out how best to get the learner to the level of desired comprehension. To organize instructional activities, pre-testing plays a key role to design an effective instruction. If an effective instruction is designed well, instructional goals will be achieved successfully.

Define the Outputs

Finally, the outputs must be defined. This process involves testing and analysis of results. This designer must implement assessment tools to determine whether the learners have adequately demonstrated the skills, knowledge, and attitudes that are described in the instructional goals and objectives. When the students participate in the instructional activities, the teachers want to know whether they learned what the instructional plan expected them to learn. To determine student learning, an appropriate educational measurement and evaluation process must be implemented. This process gives instructors results on what students learn from the instruction. In a fully self-contained learning environment, this is imperative in that there is no human intervention in the process of analyzing learner performance feedback.

The feedback process involves revising the environment based upon the actual learner results as compared to the required results. While the environment is self-contained, there is the opportunity to revise materials when the environment is initially tested. There also may be periodic revisions. If the designer during the feedback phase finds that students are not learning what the planned instruction intended, and/or they are not engaged, a revision may be warranted.

Example Application

Inputs

In assessing the website, the targeted audience and subject matter is middle school science/math (grades 7 and 8). The specific science field will be math and physics as they relate to knots and knot tying. Another targeted audience can be the sailing community or people interested from the perspective of general knowledge. Figure 1.1 depicts the main website page.

Processing

The students will be shown a website that discusses knots from both an historical and a technical perspective.

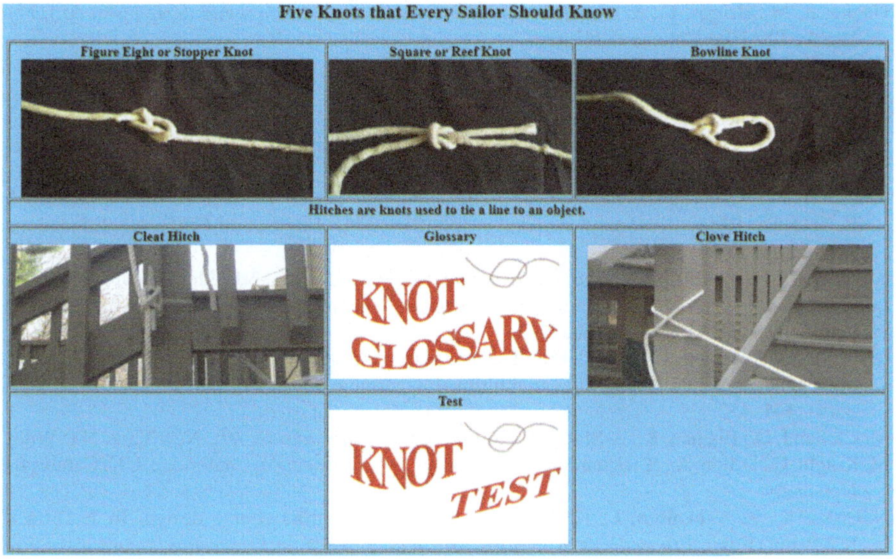

Fig. 1.1 The main page of the website

Outputs

A quiz will be administered at each section of the site quiz to determine the degree of understanding that the student has attained.

References

Baecker, R., & Small, I. (1995). Animation at the interface. In B. Laurel (Ed.), *The art of human-computer interface design*. Reading, MA: Addison-Wesley.

Beeman, W. O., Anderson, K. T., Bader, G., Larking, J., McClard, A. P., McQuillan, P., & Shields, M. (1987). Hypertext and pluralism: From linear to non-linear thinking. In J. B. Smith, F. Halasz, N. Yankelovich, M. Schwartz, & F. Weiss (Eds.), *Hypertext '87* (pp. 67–81). Chapel Hill, NC: University of North Carolina.

Berg, G. (2000). Human-computer interaction (HCI) in educational environments: Implications of understanding computers as media. *Journal of Educational Multimedia and Hypermedia, 9*(4), 347–368. Charlottesville, VA: AACE.

Davidson-Shivers, A. G. V., & Rasmussen, K. L. (2018). *Web-based learning: Design, implementation, and evaluation* (2nd ed.). Upper Saddle River, NJ: Springer.

Dove, I. (2011). Visual analogies and arguments. In F. Zenker (Ed.), *Argumentation: Cognition and community. Proceedings of the 9th international conference of the Ontario Society for the Study of Argumentation (OSSA)*, May 18–21, 2011. Windsor, ON (CD ROM) (pp. 1–16).

Driscoll, M. P. (2005). *Psychology of learning for instruction* (pp. 384–407, Chap. 11-Constructivism). Toronto, ON: Pearson.

Gagne, R. M., Briggs, L., & Wager, W. (1992). *Principles of instructional design* (4th ed.). Fort Worth, TX: HBJ College Publishers.

Gagne, R. M., Wager, W. W., Golas, K. G., & Keller, J. M. (2005). *Principles of instructional design*. Toronto, ON: Thomson Wadsworth.

Hunt, E. B. (1978). Mechanics of verbal ability. *Psychological Review, 85*(2), 109–130.

Isman, A. (2005). The implementation results of new instructional design model: Isman model. *Turkish Online Journal of Educational Technology, 4*(4), 7.

Jones, M. G., & Farquhar, J. D. (1997). User interface design for web-based instruction. In B. H. Khan (Ed.), *Web-based instruction* (pp. 239–244). Englewood Cliffs, NJ: Educational Technology Publication.

Khan, B. H. (Ed.). (1997). *Web-based instruction*. Englewood Cliffs, NJ: Educational Technology.

Lohr, L. (2003). *Creating graphics for learning and performance: Lessons in visual literacy*. Columbus, OH: Merrill Prentice Hall.

Mayer, R. E., & Anderson, R. B. (1992). The instructive animation: Helping students build connections between words and pictures in multimedia learning. *Journal of Educational Psychology, 84*(4), 444–452.

McClelland, D., Eisman, K., & Stone, T. (2000). *Web design studio secrets*. New York, NY: Wiley.

McKnight, C., Dillon, A., & Richardson, J. (1991). *Hypertext in context*. Cambridge, UK: Cambridge University.

Nakaska, K., & VanDusen, C. (2017). Best practices in online course design. In J. Dron & S. Mishra (Eds.), *Proceedings of E-learn: World conference on E-learning in corporate, government, healthcare, and higher education* (pp. 416–419). Vancouver, BC: Association for the Advancement of Computing in Education (AACE).

Nielsen, J. (2000). *Designing web usability: The practice of simplicity*. Indianapolis, IN: New Riders Publishing.

Norman, D. A. (1998). *The invisible computer: Why good products can fail, the PC is so complex, and information appliances the answer*. Cambridge, MA: MIT Press.

Osgood, R. E. (1994). The conceptual indexing of conversational hypertext (Technical Report #52). Evanston, IL: Institute for the Learning Sciences, Northwestern University.

Saxena, A., Kothari, D., Jain, S., & Khurana, A. (2002). Understanding consumer navigation behavior. *Journal of Educational Multimedia and Hypermedia, 11*(4), 403–417. Norfolk, VA: AACE.

Shneiderman, B. (1993). Education by engagement and construction: Experiences in the AT&T teaching theater. Keynote for ED-MEDIA93, Orlando, FL. In H. Maurer (Ed.), *Educational multimedia and hypermedia annual* (pp. 471–479). Charlottesville, VA: Association for the Advancement of Computing in Education.

Shneiderman, B., et al. (2016). Designing the user interface: Strategies for effective human-computer interaction, 6th, Addison-Wesley, Reading, MA.

Zhu, M., Bonk, C. J., & Sari, A. (2017). Instructor experiences in designing and delivering interactive MOOCs in higher education. In J. Dron & S. Mishra (Eds.), *Proceedings of E-learn: World conference on E-learning in corporate, government, healthcare, and higher education* (pp. 509–515). Vancouver, BC: Association for the Advancement of Computing in Education (AACE).

Zhu, L., & Grabowski, B. (2006). Web-based animation or static graphics: Is the extra cost of animation worth it? *Journal of Educational Multimedia and Hypermedia, 15*(3), 329–347. Chesapeake, VA: AACE.

Chapter 2
Theory and Practice

Cognitive Underpinnings

Vu Minh and Herbst (2008) argue that Web-based and interactive multimedia technologies especially animations and slideshows can create a learning environment supporting cognitive flexibility for pre-service secondary mathematics teachers to learn about choosing the givens for a scenario in geometry instruction.

Another theory that can used to guide a learning environment is B. F. Skinner's theory of behaviorism. Skinner promoted an approach to psychology and learning that is centered on behavior (Skinner, 1987). Skinner's position is that learning can be understood, explained, and predicted by the observable behavior of the learner along with their environmental cues for appropriate behavior and subsequent consequences which dictate whether the behavior has been learned and should be repeated.

For example, a learner whose behavior is rewarded with a good grade for doing extra assignments in class will be more likely to perform extra work in the future than one whose behavior goes unnoticed. Likewise, a learner who devises a new navigation pattern for finding information in a learning environment is more likely to continue using it if it proves to be successful and therefore reinforced (Laureano-Cruces, Sanchez-Guerrero, Velasco-Santos, & Mora-Torres, 2017).

B. F. Skinner and his supporters investigated the principles of behavior modification in their research. They tested them in instructional applications which have had significant impact on the instructional design field. Behavioral learning theory is experimental so that behavior is observed both before and after some instruction has been implemented. The observed changes in performance are related to what occurred during the instruction. If there is no behavioral change, the intervention is considered ineffective. In the instructional design field, observations are an integral part of evaluation. It collects information about whether instruction resulted in learning (behavioral change) and how improvements optimize learner performance (Reiser & Dempsey, 2007).

J. Frantiska Jr., *Interface Development for Learning Environments*,
SpringerBriefs in Educational Communications and Technology,
https://doi.org/10.1007/978-3-030-14482-1_2

With the emphasis on the learner's behavior in this theory, concepts such as behavioral objectives and the importance of practice in instruction are brought to the forefront. Before the start of instruction, teachers can see whether learners have acquired a required behavior through observation. Required behaviors that are not exhibited can be specified as learning outcomes and addressed during instruction. Required behaviors as objectives also require that learners have sufficient opportunities to practice them.

The final part in the sequence of instruction is feedback. When learners respond correctly during instruction, immediate feedback that the answer was correct is expected to reinforce the response and complete the learning process. Similarly, feedback that an answer was incorrect is expected to reduce the occurrence of incorrect responses. Historically, designers broke instruction into small portions and mandated frequent answers (Holland & Skinner, 1961) in hopes that errors would be eliminated. However, these designs were found to be boring by learners, who would look ahead at answers before they responded.

The informational value of feedback became apparent when researchers and practitioners began to adopt the perspective of information-processing theory in the 1970s. One of the principles of information-processing theory is that development is driven by self-modification so for accurate learning to take place, immediate and informative feedback is imperative. Like behaviorism, information-processing theory regards the environment to be important in learning. However, it differs in that its assumption of internal processes within the learner that explains learning.

Atkinson and Shiffrin (1968) proposed a three stage theory of memory that serves as the basis for information-processing theory. Three memory systems in the learner (sensory, short-term, and long-term memory) are assumed to receive information from the environment and transform it for storage and use in memory and performance.

- Information enters the human information-processing system through a variety of channels coupled with the various senses. Due to a limited processing ability, some incoming information can't be immediately dealt with. This information is contained momentarily in a temporary form of memory and processed later. This is what some call the "back of my memory" and is formerly known as *sensory memory*.
- Information that is processed is held in another temporary form of memory called *short-term or working memory*. A person is aware of and can work with information in working memory. Information that is held in working memory is very volatile as it tends to decay as soon as it is no longer attended to (approximately 18–20 s). Information that is the focus of attention of the information-processing system may become represented more permanently in a process referred to as *storage*. Information that is not more permanently stored is lost shortly after attention is directed elsewhere. This limited capacity of working memory causes it to be described as the *bottleneck* of the human information-processing system.
- *Long-term memory* is a more permanent form of memory that can retain information that is not being attended to. Storing information in long-term memory is equivalent to a computer writing information out to its hard drive. The recording process is called *storage* and the "playback" process, *retrieval*.
- Long-term memory's capacity is virtually unlimited in the sense that no one seems to run out of the capacity to store new information, even if they live beyond

100 years. It is difficult to determine how long memories can exist in long-term memory. If you cannot remember something you once knew, is it because it has been lost from the system, or because you have developed a problem locating it for retrieval? You may be unable to remember someone's name at present, for example, but later it is needed. Obviously, it was there in memory all the while.

The purpose of feedback from an information-processing viewpoint is twofold. First, it informs the learner with the degree of correctness of his response. The second function of feedback provides corrective information that the learner can use to modify his response. In this way, feedback can be used to continually modify what is stored in memory and used to guide performance.

To assist learners in processing information in a learning environment, designers have incorporated strategies into their instructional designs that direct attention, assist retrieval, and provide practice. The use of boldface, blinking, and italic print in text materials can draw learners' attention to important information just as the use of color in diagrams or slides can help them distinguish important features of visual information. Diagrams and images can help learners create connections between their prior knowledge and the new information they are learning. Finally, providing many kinds of examples or problems in different contexts can help learners apply the knowledge they are acquiring to situations where it is relevant (Atkinson & Shiffrin, 1968).

We must ensure that the representation of information at the interface is compatible with the learner's cognitive processes and perceptual senses. The choice of structures and overlays in the composition of e-learning frames reflects a deep understanding of the established cognitive models to engage the learner on the key pedagogic elements rather than distract them (Frantiska, 2004).

If employing Spiro's cognitive flexibility theory, one learns akin to "criss-crossing conceptual landscapes." Issues involved are analyzed in different contexts and from different perspectives. The instructional medium makes such criss-crossing possible and knowledge representations reflect the "criss-crossing that occurred during learning." The criss-crossing nature leads to knowledge structures that can be likened to a Web-like form. This implication of high interconnectivity accounts for flexibility in application. Such structures can be easily re-assembled for problem-solving in new domains. Hypermedia is particularly well-suited to impart these knowledge structures (Frantiska, 2001).

Dual Coding

Dual-coding theory (Paivio, 1986, 1991) explains concreteness effects by recourse to modality-specific systems for representation and processing. According to this theory, a variant of the multiple semantic-systems view, concrete words are associated with information stored in both a verbal "linguist" semantic system and a nonverbal "imagistic" semantic system.

Abstract words, however, are associated primarily with information stored in the linguistic system. When one encounters a concrete word it initially activates linguistic information, but shortly thereafter it also begins to activate imagistic information via referential links that interconnect the linguistic and image systems. Abstract words, on the other hand, lack or have many fewer referential connections between systems and predominantly activate linguistic representations. Concrete words have distinct processing advantages over abstract words because they have access to information from multiple systems. For example, in a lexical decision task participants can classify "hand" as a word faster than "idea" because "hand" is processed and represented in both systems, while "idea" is processed/represented only in the linguistic system. This additional semantic activity from dual systems allows participants to quickly differentiate concrete words from pseudo-words (pseudo-words presumably generate little semantic activation). The relatively lower semantic activity from a single system makes abstract words more difficult to differentiate from pseudo-words resulting in relatively slower reaction times.

Dissonance Theory

Along with the non-selectivity of what information the learner exposes himself to, there will be a lack of resistance to accepting and cognizing any relevant information. Prior to the taking of action, many cognitive elements will have been established which may later be dissonant with the cognition corresponding to the action which does ensure (Festinger, 1957).

One may say that the pre-action or pre-decision situation will be characterized by extended and non-selective seeking of relevant information. Of course, it is rather rare that there is a pure pre-action situation. Most instances will involve mixtures. For example, a person who has decided to purchase a car but has not decided which type of car will seek out information about various aspects of cars. He will be selective so that he will be exposed to information which would be dissonant with his decision to purchase a car.

The presence or absence of dissonance in some content area will have important effects on the degree of information seeking and on the selectivity of such information seeking. If dissonance exists between two cognitive elements or between two clusters of cognitive elements, it may be reduced by adding new cognitive elements which produce new consonant relationships. One would then expect that in the presence of dissonance, one would observe the information which might reduce the existing dissonance.

The behavior one would observe on the part of a person with no dissonance would be identical with the behavior of the person for whom no relevance to any present or future behavior. There is an important difference in that for the latter person, accidental exposure will not introduce dissonance, while for the former who does not avoid sources of information, dissonance may be accidentally introduced.

There are distinct degrees of dissonance:

1. *Relative absence of dissonance.* If little or no dissonance exists, there would be no motivation (considering this source of motivation alone) to seek out new and

additional information. There would also be little or no motivation to avoid any source of information. Thus, in the example of a car purchase, if a person had recently purchased a car but had no cognitive dissonance, this person would not be inclined to either acquire information or to avoid it. What is important is that if there is really an absence of dissonance, this lack of motivation to acquire or avoid the information would be quite independent of the car he had just purchased.

2. *The presence of moderate amounts of dissonance.* The existence of appreciable dissonance and the consequent pressure to reduce it will lead to the seeking out of information which will introduce consonances and to the avoidance of information which will increase the already existing dissonance. When faced with a potential source of information, a person usually does not know the exact nature of the cognition that he would acquire from exposure to this information source. He must then react in terms of expectations about it. If he is led to expect it will produce cognitions that will increase consonance, he will expose himself to the information source. If the expectation is that the cognition acquired through this source would increase dissonance, he will avoid it. Under most circumstances this kind of action to reduce dissonance is a rather fallible procedure. To the extent that one's expectations may prove wrong, an attempt at dissonance reduction may have the unfortunate result of increasing dissonance.

   For example, a person who has recently purchased a new car notices the announcement of a lecture on high horsepower automotive engines. One would expect him to be inclined to attend the lecture if the car he has recently purchased has a powerful engine. The title of the lecture would lead him to expect that he would obtain cognition that would be compatible with having purchased the car he now owns. If he had purchased a car with low power, one would expect him to avoid the lecture. This would not simply be a matter of indifference but of active avoidance.

   The limit of dissonance that can possibly exist between any two elements is equal to the total resistance to change of the less resistant element. The magnitude of dissonance can't exceed this amount because, at this point of maximum possible dissonance, the less resistant element would change, thus eliminating the dissonance. What might one say about seeking out new information by a person whose dissonance is near the limit? Under such circumstances a person may actively seek out and expose himself to dissonance-increasing information. If he can increase the dissonance to the point where it is greater than the resistance to change of one or another cluster of cognitions, he will then change the cognitive elements involved, thus markedly reducing or perhaps even wholly eliminating the dissonance that now is so great.

3. *The presence of extremely large amounts of dissonance.* Let us recall that there is a limit to the magnitude of dissonance that can exist in a system. If two cognitive elements exist in a dissonant relationship, the maximum magnitude this dissonance can have is equal to the resistance to change of the less resistant element of the pair. Similarly, if dissonance exists between one group of elements and another group, this dissonance cannot exceed in magnitude the resistance to

change of the least resistant parts of the groups. If the dissonance becomes greater than the resistance to change, then the least resistant elements of cognition will be changed and reduce the dissonance.

The limit of dissonance is related to the pioneering work of George A. Miller in his seminal article "The Magical Number Seven, Plus or Minus Two: Some Limits on Our Capacity for Processing Information." He states "We give the observer as much time as he wants to make his response; we simply increase the number of alternative stimuli among which he must discriminate and look to see where confusions begin to occur. Confusions will appear near the point that we are calling his 'channel capacity'" (Miller, 1956).

Learning Taxonomies

Taxonomy is the practice and science of classification and is usually arranged in a hierarchical structure. Typically, this is organized by supertype–subtype relationships, e.g., parent–child relationships. Three types of learning have been analyzed and represented as taxonomies: cognitive (thinking), affective (valuing and appreciating), and psychomotor (physical movement). In a learning taxonomy, there are different levels. One learns at one level before advancing to the next level, and mastery of a higher level depends on the ability to learn at the lower level (Shambaugh & Magliaro, 2006).

Cognitive Learning Taxonomy

Educational psychologist Benjamin S. Bloom devised a classification of educational objectives based on cognitive complexity called Bloom's taxonomy (Fig. 2.1). It can aid teachers and designers to create objectives and derive appropriate measures of learned capability and higher order thinking skills (Bloom, 1956).

If the type of learning required of the student includes the recall of new information, the cognitive level of learning is "knowledge." For example, if you recite a passage from a play, the complexity of thinking grows more challenging as you reach the next level of "Comprehension." At this level you must understand, that is, comprehend; the meaning, translation, interpolation, and interpretation of instructions and problems. At this level you may be required to explain in your own words the steps for performing a complex task. At the next level of "Application," you will continue to move farther away from rote recitation and be expected to use a learned concept in a new situation. Progressing even farther away is the next level of "Analysis" where you may be required to breakdown concepts into their component parts so that its organizational structure may be understood. The next level of "Synthesis" is where the learner may be required to construct a new, complete

Category	Learner Behavior and Keywords
Knowledge: Recall data or information.	**Learner Behaviors:** Recite a poem. Recall stock prices from memory. Know the procedure for CPR. **Keywords:** defines, describes, identifies, knows, labels, lists, names, outlines, recalls, recite, reproduces, selects.
Comprehension: Understand the meaning, translation, and interpretation of instructions and problems. State a problem in one's own words.	**Learner Behaviors:** Rewrites the principles of poetry writing Explain in one's own words the steps for performing CPR. Translates stock quotes into another currency. **Keywords:** comprehends, converts, defends, distinguishes, estimates, explains, extends, generalizes, gives Learner Behaviors, infers, interprets, paraphrases, predicts, rewrites, summarizes, translates.
Application: Use a concept in a new situation or unprompted use of an abstraction.	**Learner Behaviors:** Use a manual to perform CPR. Apply laws of statistics to evaluate the reliability of a stock quote. **Keywords:** applies, changes, computes, constructs, demonstrates, discovers, manipulates, modifies, operates, predicts, prepares, produces, relates, shows, solves, uses.
Analysis: Separates material or concepts into component parts so that its organizational structure may be understood. Distinguishes between facts and inferences.	**Learner Behaviors:** Analyze logical fallacies in poetry. Gaters information from a manual and selects the required tasks for CPR training. **Keywords:** analyzes, breaks down, compares, contrasts, diagrams, deconstructs, differentiates, discriminates, distinguishes, identifies, illustrates, infers, outlines, relates, selects, separates.
Synthesis: Builds a structure or pattern from diverse elements. Put parts together to form a whole, which creates a new meaning or structure.	**Learner Behaviors:** Write a CPR procedural manual. Design a program to write poetry. Revises and process to improve the outcome of stock quote calculation. **Keywords:** categorizes, combines, compiles, composes, creates, devises, designs, explains, generates, modifies, organizes, plans, rearranges, reconstruts, relates, reorganizes, revises, rewrites, summarizes, tells, writes.
Evaluation: Make judgments about the value of ideas or materials.	**Learner Behaviors:** Select the most effective verses of a poem. Hire the most qualified CPR instructor candidate. Explain and justify a new stock quote calculation. **Keywords:** appraises, compares, concludes, contrasts, criticizes, critiques, defends, describes, discriminates, evaluates, explains, interprets, justifies, relates, summarizes, supports.

Fig. 2.1 The cognitive learning taxonomy. The more complex the level, the more it is supported and dependent upon the lesser complex levels

concept from existing diverse elements. Each successive level has required the learner to become more abstract and complex in their thinking.

The highest level of this taxonomy is "Evaluation," the capability to compare and contrast, to argue, and to decide. The learner may be required to make judgments about the value of ideas or materials such as selecting the best solution to a problem among several candidate solutions. In developing lessons and units, it is helpful to look at one's choice of student learning outcomes and see where they lie on the taxonomy. You get a sense for what you are expecting students to learn and can then make informed choices on teaching and assessment.

Affective Learning Taxonomy

If the learning environment's content includes developing attitudes or values, then the affective taxonomy can help you understand the development of this type of learning (Krathwohl, Bloom, & Masia, 1964). The affective taxonomy is organized according to the degree of personal internalization of a new idea or concept (Fig. 2.2).

Here a person's attitude shifts from general awareness of an issue to an attitude that consistently guides one's behavior. At the simplest level of "Receiving Phenomena," the learner is expected to exhibit an awareness of an issue including a willingness to hear and be able to selectively focus their attention on an area of a learning environment. Going to the next level of "Responding to Phenomena," the learner would be expected to react to a specific phenomenon with a learning environment. Learning objectives may emphasize compliance, willingness, or satisfaction in responding. The next level of "Valuing" is of a largely attitudinal nature and expects the learner to assign worth or value to a particular object, phenomenon, or behavior within the environment. The next level is "organization" and requires the learner to organize values into priorities by contrasting different values, resolving conflicts between them, and creating a unique value system. Within the context of a learning environment, the learner separates and groups concepts and/or objects with regard to their own ranking system. The final and most sophisticated level is that of "internalizing values." It is here that a learner is expected to use an objective approach in problem solving.

Psychomotor Learning Taxonomy

If the learning environments' content requires physical skills, the psychomotor domain is appropriate (Fig. 2.3). Among the various versions, Elizabeth Simpson developed a psychomotor taxonomy in 1972 which illustrates how physical skills can be analyzed and better understood, so that teachers can properly support

Category	Learner Behavior and Keywords
Receiving Phenomena: Awareness, willingness to hear, selected attention.	**Learner Behaviors:** Listen to others with respect. Listen for and remember the name of newly introduced people. **Keywords:** asks, chooses, describes, follows, gives, holds, identifies, locates, names, points to, selects, sits, erects, replies, uses.
Responding to Phenomena: Active participation on the part of the learners. Reacts to a particular phenomenon. Learning outcomes may emphasize compliance in responding, or willingness to respond (motivation)	**Learner Behaviors:** Participates in class discussions. Gives a presentation. Questions new concepts, models etc. to fully understand them. **Keywords:** answers, assists, aids, complies, conforms, discusses, greets, helps, labels, performs, practices, presents, reads, recites, reports, selects, tells, writes.
Valuing: The value a person's value is attached to a particular object, phenomenon, or behavior. Valuing is based on the internalization of a set of specified values which are expressed in the learner's overt behavior.	**Learner Behaviors:** Is sensitive towards individual and cultural differences. Shows the ability to solve problems. Proposes a plan and follows through with commitment. **Keywords:** completes, demonstrates, differentiates, explains, follows, forms, initiates, invites, joins, justifies, proposes, reads, reports, selects, shares, studies, works.
Organization: Prioritizes values by contrasting, different values, resolves conflicts, and creates a unique value system.	**Learner Behaviors:** Accepts responsibility for one's behavior. Explains the role of systematic planning in solving problems. Accepts professional ethical standards. Creates a life plan in harmony with abilities, interests, and beliefs. Prioritizes time effectively to meet the needs of the organization, family, and self. **Keywords:** adheres, alters, arranges, combines, compares, completes, defends, explains, formulates, generalizes, identifies, integrates, modifies, orders, organizes, prepares, relates, synthesizes.
Internalizing values: Their behavior is controlled by a value system. Learning objectives are concerned with the student's general patterns of adjustment (personal, social, emotional).	**Learner Behaviors:** Shows self-reliance when working independently. Cooperates in group activities (displays teamwork). Uses an objective approach in problem solving. Displays a professional commitment to ethical practice on daily basis. Revises judgments and changes behavior in light of new evidence. Values people for what they are, not how they look. **Keywords:** acts, discriminates, displays, influences, listens, modifies, performs, practices, proposes, qualifies, questions, revises, serves, solves, verifies.

Fig. 2.2 The affective learning taxonomy. It is organized according to the degree of personal internalization of a new idea or concept

Category	Learner Behavior and Keywords
Perception: The ability to use sensory cues to guide motor activity. This ranges from sensory stimulation, through cue selection, to translation.	**Learner Behaviors:** Distinguishes non-verbal communication cues. Estimates where a golf ball will land after it is hit and then moving to the correct location to recover the ball. Adjusts the angle of a computer monitor comparing the angle in relation to the line of sight. **Keywords:** chooses, describes, detects, differentiates, distinguishes, identifies, isolates, relates, selects.
Set: Mental, physical, and emotional (mind)sets. These three sets are dispositions that predetermine a person's response to different situations (sometimes called mindsets).	**Learner Behaviors:** Knows and acts upon a sequence of steps in a manufacturing process. Recognize one's abilities and limitations. Shows desire to learn a new process (motivation). **Keywords:** begins, displays, explains, moves, proceeds, reacts, shows, states, volunteers.
Guided Response: The early stages in learning a complex skill that includes imitation and trial and error. Adequacy of performance is achieved by practicing.	**Learner Behaviors:** Performs a mathematical equation as demonstrated. Follows instructions to build a model. Responds hand-signals of instructor while learning to operate a forklift. **Keywords:** copies, traces, follows, react, reproduce, responds
Mechanism: This is the intermediate stage in learning a complex skill. Learned responses have become habitual and the movements can be performed with some confidence and proficiency.	**Learner Behaviors:** Use a personal computer. Repair a leaking faucet. Drive a car. **Keywords:** assembles, calibrates, constructs, dismantles, displays, fastens, fixes, grinds, heats, manipulates, measures, mends, mixes, organizes, sketches.
Complex Overt Response: The skillful performance of motor acts that involve complex movement patterns. Proficiency is indicated by a quick, accurate, and highly coordinated performance, requiring a minimum of energy. This category includes performing without hesitation, and automatic performance.	**Learner Behaviors:** Maneuvers a car into a tight parallel parking spot. Operates a computer quickly and accurately. Displays competence while playing the piano. **Keywords:** assembles, builds, calibrates, constructs, dismantles, displays fastens, fixes, grinds, heats, manipulates, measures, mends, mixes, organizes, sketches.
Adaptation: Skills are well developed and the individual can modify movement patterns to fit special requirements.	**Learner Behaviors:** Responds effectively to unexpected experiences. Modifies instruction to meet the needs of the learners. Perform a task with a machine that it was not originally intended to do (machine is not damaged and there is no danger in performing the new task). **Keywords:** adapts, alters, changes, rearranges, reorganizes, revises, varies.

Fig. 2.3 The psychomotor learning taxonomy. The more complex the level, the more it is supported and dependent upon the lesser complex levels

learning in these skills. The degree of physical coordination required in a task is what the elements of this psychomotor taxonomy are ordered by Simpson (1972).

The lowest ordered level is Perception, which according to Simpson is "the process of becoming aware of objects, qualities, or relations by way of the sense organs." Simpson further breaks down perception into three subdivisions. The first is sensory stimulation which is stimulation of one or more of the senses: auditory, visual, tactile, taste, smell, or kinesthetic. Second is cue selection which is the decision of what cues to respond to so that the required task can be performed. The final subdivision is translation which is the relating of perception to action so that a physical task can be accomplished. Specifically, in a learning environment concerning trajectories of a thrown football (with or without a spiral motion) a learner may have to estimate where a ball will land after it is thrown as it traverses the screen and then moving to the correct location to catch the ball.

The next element of the psychomotor domain is Set which applies to having a readiness to act as in "ready, set ... go!" This element of the psychomotor domain is closely related with the "Responding to Phenomena" level of the affective domain which applies to have a willingness to respond. Both levels deal with an anticipation and preparation prior to an action. The learner would be expected to react to a specific phenomenon within a learning environment. The set can be of three possible types: mental, physical, or emotional. The next element is "guided response" which is of a largely attitudinal nature and expects the learner to assign worth or value to an object, phenomenon, or behavior within the environment. Guided response according to Simpson is "the overt behavioral act of an individual under the guidance of the instructor."

Guided response can be in the form of imitation or trial and error. The next element of the Simpson psychomotor domain is Mechanism and it is at this point that skill has become habitualized for the learner. Within the context of a learning environment, the learner has developed a repertoire of responses to stimuli and can select the most appropriate one for the given situation. The final and most sophisticated element is that of Complex Overt Response. It is here that a learner has attained a high degree of skill and actions can be performed with efficiency and smoothly. This element is further divided into Resolution of Uncertainty and Automatic Performance. Resolution of Uncertainty is when the learner is aware of the sequence of action to take to complete the task and can do so with confidence. Automatic Performance is when the learner can perform a finely coordinate physical skill easily with a high degree of muscle control.

Combining Taxonomies

Some tasks, such as writing a book or creating a prototype device, may require the use of all three taxonomies. To write a book requires a range of cognitive abilities, plus the motor skills to use a keyboard. The cognitive and affective taxonomies figure prominently in the performance of any high-level critical thinking or problem-solving task. Gagne combined all three taxonomies to create his "Learned Capabilities" taxonomy to help educators think about the relationships between the three taxonomies (Gagne, Wager, Golas, & Keller, 2005).

Once it is known that a task within a learning environment involves multiple learning types, the sequence of action that can accomplish various required tasks can be developed according to the taxonomy. Teachers frequently characterize teaching as a flow of activity, but this flow is usually based on some rationale, such as simple concepts or skills to more complex concepts or skills. Understanding the nature of what students will learn, possibly using the hierarchical arrangement provided by a taxonomy, provides a tool to establish a learner-focused rationale to the flow of teaching (Shambaugh & Magliaro, 1997).

Example Application

The taxonomy to be used is cognitive learning. This was chosen since the most important aspects of the website will require a student to remember and understand various aspects of the subject matter. Remembering and understanding are of the most important portions of the cognitive domain.

The learning theory to be used is behaviorism. This theory was selected since it emphasizes observable response to various stimuli and views all behaviors as learned by interacting with the environment. Another advantage of behaviorism is the ability to measure learning in a direct manner.

References

Atkinson, R. C., & Shiffrin, R. M. (1968). Chapter: Human memory: A proposed system and its control processes. In K. W. Spence & J. T. Spence (Eds.), *The psychology of learning and motivation* (Vol. 2, pp. 89–195). New York, NY: Academic Press.

Bloom, B. S. (Ed.). (1956). *Taxonomy of educational objectives, the classification of educational goals – Handbook I: Cognitive domain*. New York, NY: McKay.

Festinger, L. (1957). *A theory of cognitive dissonance*. Evanston, IL: Row, Peterson & Company.

Frantiska, J. J. (2001). *Misconception to concept: Employing cognitive flexibility theory-based hypermedia to promote conceptual change in ill-structured domains* (Doctoral dissertation). University of Massachusetts-Amherst.

Frantiska, J. J. (2004). From pebbles to boulders: Information chunking in educational websites. *E-learn 04' Conference*, Washington, DC, November 2, 2004.

Gagné, R. M., Wager, W. W., Golas, K. C., & Keller, J. M. (2005). *Principles of instructional design*. Belmont, CA: Wadsworth/ Thomson Learning.

Holland, J. G., & Skinner, B. F. (1961). *The analysis of behavior*. New York, NY: McGraw-Hill.

Krathwohl, D. R., Bloom, B. S., & Masia, B. B. (1964). *Taxonomy of educational objectives, book 2: Affective domain*. New York, NY: Longman.

Laureano-Cruces, A. L., Sanchez-Guerrero, L., Velasco-Santos, P., & Mora-Torres, M. (2017). The interface: An object that is hated and loved. In J. Dron & S. Mishra (Eds.), *Proceedings of E-learn: World conference on E-learning in corporate, government, healthcare, and higher education* (pp. 380–388). Vancouver, BC: Association for the Advancement of Computing in Education (AACE). Retrieved June 7, 2018, from https://www.learntechlib.org/primary/p/181208/

Miller, G. A. (1956). The magical number seven, plus or minus two. *Psychological Review, 63*, 81–97.

Paivio, A. (1986). *Mental representations*. New York, NY: Oxford University Press.

Paivio, A. (1991). Dual coding theory: Retrospect and current status. *Canadian Journal of Psychology, 45*(3), 255–287.

Reiser, R. A., & Dempsey, J. V. (Eds.). (2007). *Trends and issues in instructional design and technology* (2nd ed.). Upper Saddle River, NJ: Pearson Education.

Shambaugh, R. N., & Magliaro, S. G. (1997). *Mastering the possibilities: A process approach to instructional design*. Boston, MA: Allyn & Bacon.

Shambaugh, N., & Magliaro, S. G. (2006). *Instructional design: A systematic approach for reflective practice*. Boston, MA: Allyn and Bacon.

Simpson, E. J. (1972). *The classification of educational objectives in the psychomotor domain*. Washington, DC: Gryphon House.

Skinner, B. F. (1987). A thinking aid. *Journal of Applied Behavior Analysis, 20*, 379–380.

Vu Minh, C., & Herbst, P. (2008). Learning to teach: Web-based interactive rich-media technologies supporting cognitive flexibility in teacher education. In K. McFerrin et al. (Eds.), *Proceedings of society for information technology & teacher education international conference 2008* (pp. 4579–4586). Chesapeake, VA: AACE.

Chapter 3
Development

Elaboration Theory

One of the methodologies available for this purpose is elaboration theory (ET) first proposed by Charles Reigeluth then of Syracuse University in 1979. To optimize learning according to elaboration theory, instruction along with associated materials should be organized by an increasing order of complexity. For instance, when teaching a procedure, the simplest version of the task is presented first; subsequent lessons present additional versions until the full range of tasks are taught. ET is best used to explain and explore cause-and-effect relationships as well as sequences. Facts and problem-solving are not as well served by the employment of ET (Wu, 2003).

To understand the concept of elaboration theory, a good example is using a telescope. When you first look into the telescope, you are looking at the highest level of detail, i.e., the entire night sky with the many twinkling points of light. Once you have determined the part of the sky that you want to concentrate on, the telescope can be used to zoom in to see an increasing level of detail. The points of light gradually become planets, stars, or entire clusters of stars. Your examination of the sky begins with the broadest, simplest perspective and the major relationships among the major parts of that perspective (the overview), without delving into the detail. As you zoom in on one area of the sky, more detail (the *elaboration*) is exposed. After each level of detail, the learner needs to be reminded of all previous levels seen (Reigeluth, 1999).

Based on a set of seven *strategy components*, the theory also describes how the subject matter structures are related for prescribing various possible instructional sequences. In ET, a strategy is created by combining the different components in different ways. The seven strategy components described in (Reigeluth, 1999) are:

1. *Elaborative sequence of major tasks (either conceptual, procedural, or theoretical).* Break down tasks into their subtasks of lesser complexity to analyze the structure and reveal the inherent complexity of the parent task.

J. Frantiska Jr., *Interface Development for Learning Environments*,
SpringerBriefs in Educational Communications and Technology,
https://doi.org/10.1007/978-3-030-14482-1_3

2. *Sequencing of learning prerequisites within individual lessons of a course.* Place learning prerequisites before new content.
3. *Summary.* Summarizing collapses complex concepts to single, easily handled concepts. This summarization can be presented by the developer or drawn from the learners as insights.
4. *Synthesis.* Synthesizing creates connectivity to previous and current learning. It allows the learner to make connections so that learners can begin to understand. These connectors may be concepts in and of themselves (depending on the complexity of the material), but normally they are simple methods that connect content (subject matter), procedures (what to do), or theories (why to do what you do).
5. *Analogies.* An analogy is the use of a familiar idea or concept to introduce or define a new idea or concept. Analogies are of two types: examples and non-examples. Examples are those where the resemblances between objects, situations, or ideas are similar, and the similarity is obvious. Non-examples are instances in which the similarities may be superficial or misleading. The combination of the two helps the learner understand how the new material is like the old as well as how they differ. Analogies aid the environment in reaching the learner's field of experience. Presenting analogies throughout the instruction helps the learners build on their present knowledge or skills.
6. *Cognitive strategies.* These strategies are cues to the learner to apply the learning skills they already have, for example, asking, "How does this relate to your past experience?"
7. *Learner control.* This provides motivation and relevance for the learner. New learners acquiring basic skills tend to need a lot of structure to facilitate learning. More advanced learners learn more quickly when they have control over their learning decisions.

The detailed prescription in ET on the various macro-strategies has also offered a wealth of terminology and descriptions for the elicitation of instructional procedures. One criticism of ET is that many concepts are sequenced from the most general perspective down to the most detailed, so elaboration theory does not accommodate learner's prior knowledge.

How can ET be used in the instructional design of a learning environment? To continue with our telescope example, let's say that we need to create an environment about the Hubble Space Telescope. We could employ ET to show learners how this device can be used to examine with increasing detail in the sky. We also could use ET in the reverse direction. For example, the analogy of a microscope could be used in a cardiology class to show the increasing levels of detail of a part of the human heart from the tissue's surface to the cellular level.

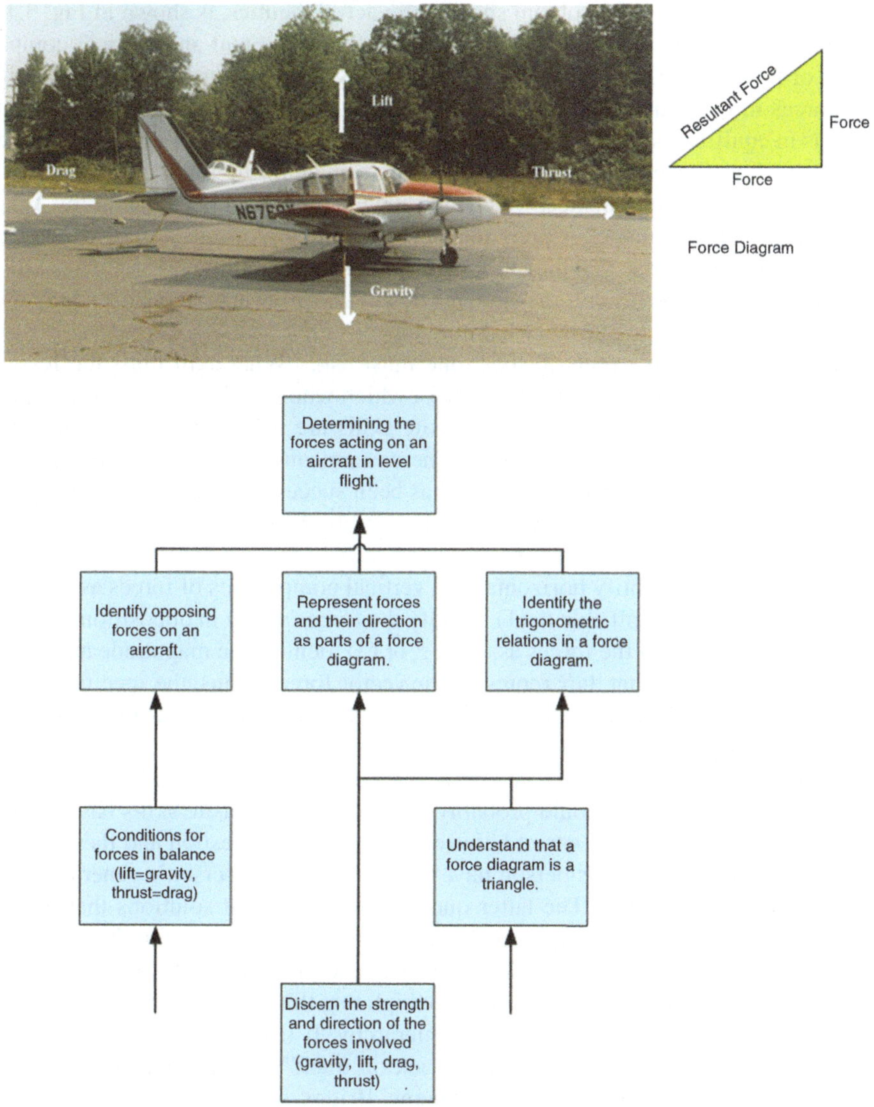

Fig. 3.1 A learning hierarchy for identifying horizontal and vertical components of forces acting on an aircraft in level flight

Learning Hierarchies

The learning hierarchy that results from a learning-task analysis is the arrangement of intellectual skill objectives into a pattern that shows the prerequisite relationships among them. An additional example of a learning hierarchy, this time for a skill in solving a type of physics problem specifically aerodynamics, is shown in Fig. 3.1.

Here, the lesson objective is one of finding the horizontal and vertical components of forces as vectors of an aircraft in level flight. They must be able to identify the forces in the situation that are acting in opposition to each other when the aircraft is in equilibrium and then represent these opposing forces as arrows in a force diagram whose length and direction are proportionate to the force described. Each of these skills has prerequisites, which are shown below them in the hierarchy. What is meant by a prerequisite? A prerequisite skill is integral to the skill to which it is subordinate in the sense that the latter skill cannot be done if the prerequisite skill is not available to the learner. If the students do not know these prerequisites, they will not be able to satisfy the primary learning objective.

To identity a skill's prerequisites, one must ask, "What skill must the learner have to learn this (new) skill, the absence of which would make that learning impossible?" (Gagne, 1985). That is, prerequisite skills are those that are critical to the rapid, smooth learning of the new skill. There is a means of checking whether a first try at answering the preceding question has been successful. This is done by examining the demands that the new skill makes on the learner and identity where he could fail. Applying this to the objective of Fig. 3.1, one can see that students who are attempting to "identify horizontal and vertical components of forces as vectors" might fail if they weren't able to (1) identify the forces acting in opposition (at equilibrium), (2) represent the forces as arrows, or (3) identify the magnitude and direction of the arrows so that they represent the vector forces. Thus, the specification of prerequisites should provide a complete description of those previously learned skills necessary for acquiring the new skill most readily.

If one finds a learner who is having trouble acquiring a new intellectual skill, the first diagnostic question should probably be, "What prerequisite skills has this person failed to learn?" The contrast between the preceding question and these "What genetic deficiency does this person have?" or "What is the person's general intelligence?" will be apparent. The latter questions may suggest solutions that merely serve to remove the learner from the learning environment by putting him or her in a social group or class. Responsible diagnosis, in contrast, attempts to discover what the learner needs to learn. The chances are high that this will be a prerequisite intellectual skill, as indicated by a learning hierarchy. If it is, suitable instruction can readily be designed to get the learner "back on track" in a learning sequence that continues to be positively reinforcing (Gagne, Briggs, & Wager, 1992).

Prototyping

The spiral model is a software development model combining elements of both design and prototyping in stages. So, what really is prototyping? This approach was not the first model to discuss iteration in software development, but it was the first model to explain why the iteration matters. Each phase starts with a design goal (such as a user interface prototype as an early phase) and ends with the client (which may be internal) reviewing the progress thus far. Analysis and engineering efforts are applied to each phase of the project, with an eye toward the end goal of the project. The spiral model lays down the foundation and, through iteration, gradually builds more administrative functionality as the project spirals into the final phase of a detailed implementation.

The spiral methodology isn't just used to rapid prototype, e.g., to look at various potential design before full scale development is undertaken. It can also be used in the development of a learning environment. For example, if you are building a house, the building process is really a form of spiral development. Specifically, the house doesn't go up all at once, it is built in iterative stages that build upon one another. First, the plot of land is cleared followed by the foundation being poured on the plot followed by the frame of the house built on the foundation and then the walls, shingles, and siding are attached to the frame.

In the same manner, a learning environment is initially laid out at a high level. In the next iteration, the portions of the environment are designed with their connectivity with each other in mind. Next, the candidate multimedia tools are examined and then the appropriate tools are selected based upon what is required of them during a learners' usage of the environment. This is not necessarily a trivial task especially as the complexity of the environment rises. All possible needs to be imposed upon the tools must be ascertained and understood prior to their selection. Once the tools are selected and placed within the environment their connectivity must be tested and the environment as a whole must be tested. Just as with the house, the learning environment evolves via an iterative process.

Storyboarding

After the idea for a learning environment has been developed, it's time to turn it into a fully functioning environment. We need to somehow "lay everything out" to see what materials we have and how we will connect them together. One tried and true way to do this is storyboarding. A storyboard is a physical or virtual device used to define each part of the environment and how it will be arranged and interact with the learner (Davidson-Shivers & Rasmussen, 2018). It is analogous to the blueprint or plot plan that the architect creates to show how the portions of the building will fit together. However, this technique has been used for years by many times of people long before the advent of computers. A director will use a storyboard artist to sketch frames of selected scenes from the writer's script. An editor will paste portions of a magazine page on a large bulletin board to see how the story will flow between text and graphics. A cartoonist will storyboard how the scenes of the cartoon will evolve, etc. They are all trying to answer the question "How can I understand the big picture and then see how the portions within it interact?" Of course, this historically has been accomplished with "old-fashioned" materials: bulletin board, paper, thumbtacks, and it has worked well for a long time.

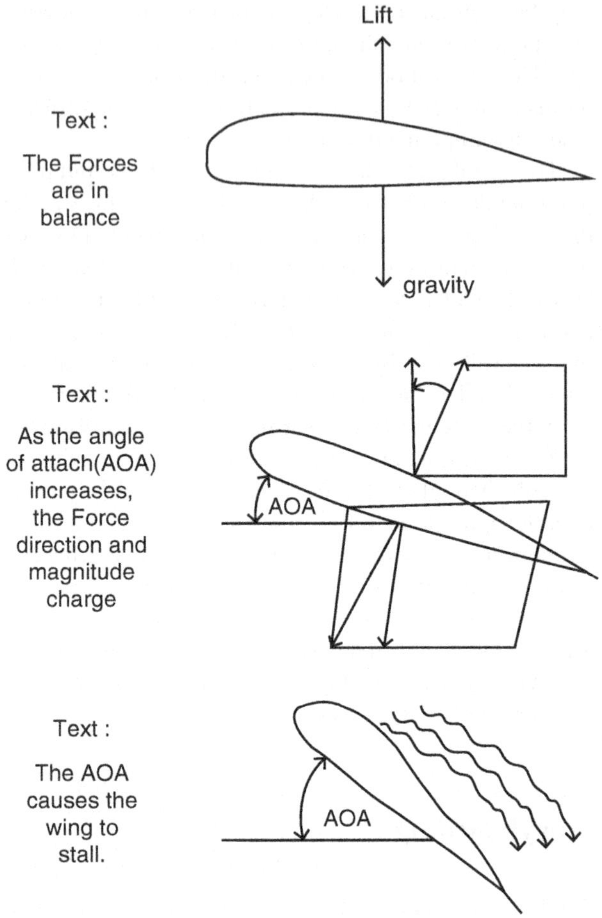

Fig. 3.2 An example of a paper and pencil storyboarding of a website

However, this process can be rather tedious and clumsy especially as the complexity of a system increases. This can be particularly true with a multiple page, hypermedia-based learning environment filled with various types of media and its complex pathways. While a storyboard can be done in a very low-tech manner with paper and pencil (Fig. 3.2), what would be helpful is a digital version of this technique that can be quickly modified in much the same way that modern tools aid the architect. An example of this is a widespread and easy to use standard tool such as Microsoft Word® (Fig. 3.3) or PowerPoint® that supports the acceptance and use of the storyboard concept for many reasons such as:

- Knowledge or information sharing with data available in other formats like XML or Microsoft Office® products such as Word® or Excel® is easy to implement. The storyboards implemented in Visio® have a high expandability. There is no need to rewrite former documents or data of the educational system to integrate their knowledge into storyboards.

<table>
<tr><td>Narration:
The basic layout of the engine.</td><td>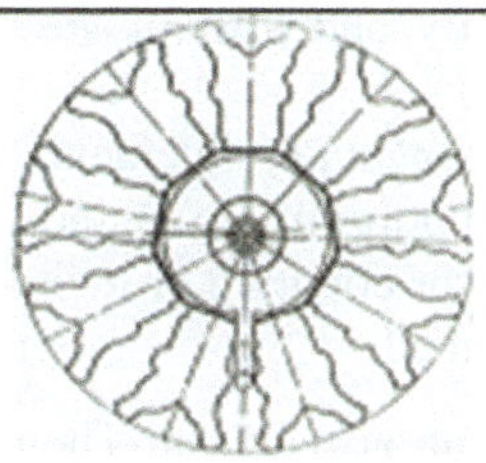</td></tr>
<tr><td>Narration:
On left are the connecting rods with the master rod in the middle. At right is a cylinder head.</td><td>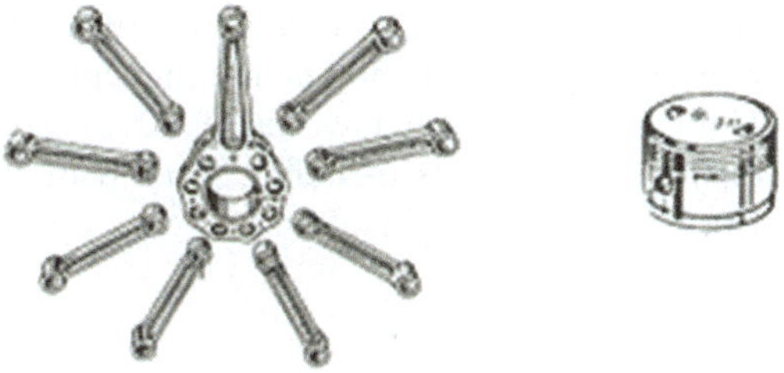</td></tr>
<tr><td>Narration:
These are the parts of the cylinder and how the piston components fit in it.</td><td>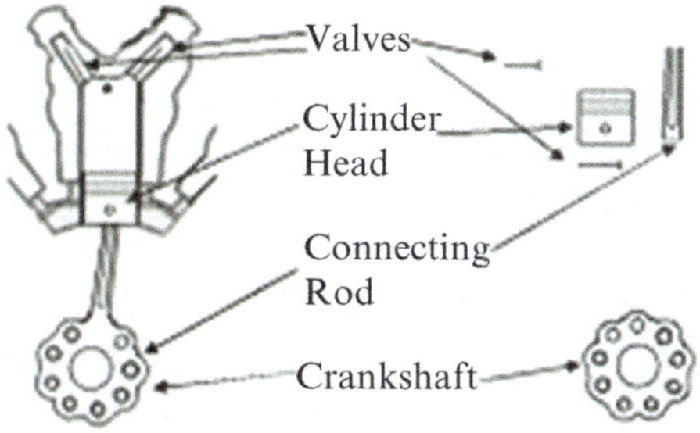
</td></tr>
<tr><td>Narration:
These are the phases in the ignition and power strokes of the combustion cycle.</td><td>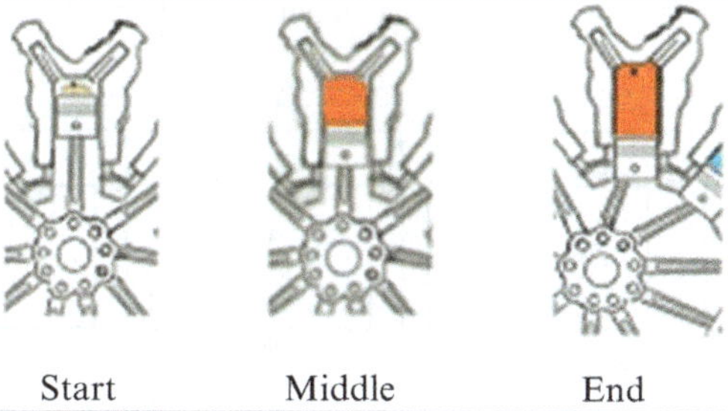
</td></tr>
<tr><td>Narration:
This the view of all cylinders as they go through the various strokes of the cycle.</td><td>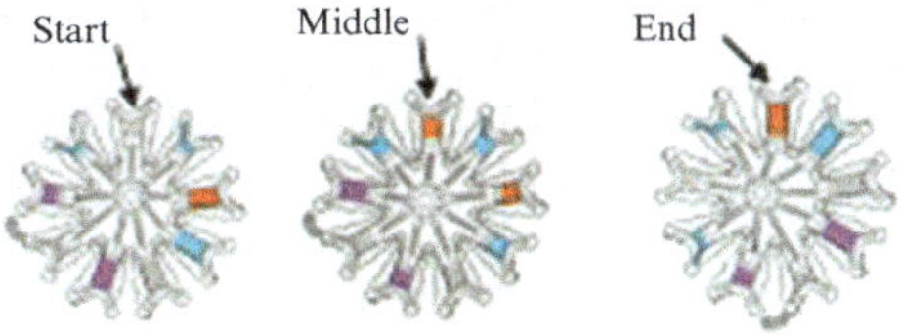
</td></tr>
</table>

Fig. 3.3 Storyboarding with a table created in Microsoft Word®

- The educational model can easily and visually be created and modified by people.
- The implementation, use, evaluation, and refinement of storyboards can be supported by computers using the opportunity to include macros in Visual Basic®. Simple consistence checks, e.g., for counting or logical mistakes by human storyboard authors, can be implemented.

The complexity of storyboards can go very far. The concept allows for deeply nested structures involving different forms of learning and permitting a large variety of alternatives. Discussions begin frequently with a top level storyboard of only about half a dozen nodes. Discussing their arrangement is a first step toward didactic design (Dohi, Sakurai, Tsuruta, & Knauf, 2006). There are currently numerous software tools for storyboarding including Storyboard Quick® and Storyboard Pro® from Toon Boom for the Apple MacIntosh®.

Example Application

The elements that will be used for the example are the learning objectives, course navigation, instructional strategies, audio cues, and quiz feedback. Due to the educational/learning object nature of the example, a linear sequencing will be used within a thread, but a hierarchical sequencing will be used within a knowledge area. Figure 3.4 depicts the basic structure of the website.

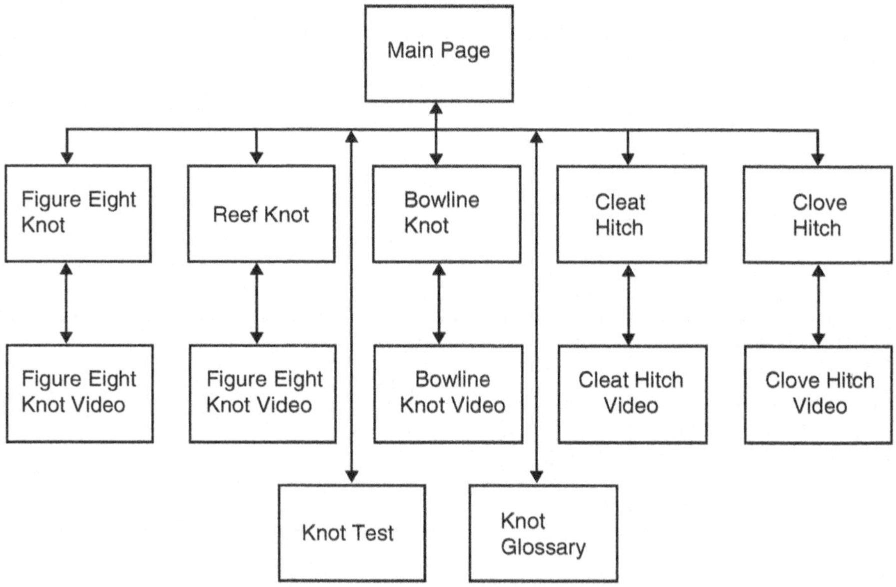

Fig. 3.4 The structure of the website

References

Davidson-Shivers, A. G. V., & Rasmussen, K. L. (2018). *Web-based learning: Design, implementation, and evaluation* (2nd ed.). Upper Saddle River, NJ: Springer.

Dohi, S., Sakurai, Y., Tsuruta, S., & Knauf, R. (2006). Managing academic education through dynamic storyboarding. In T. Reeves & S. Yamashita (Eds.), *Proceedings of world conference on E-learning in corporate, government, healthcare, and higher education 2006* (pp. 1611–1619). Chesapeake, VA: AACE.

Gagne, R. M. (1985). *The conditions of learning and theory of instruction*. New York, NY: CBS College Publishing.

Gagne, R. M., Briggs, L., & Wager, W. (1992). *Principles of instructional design* (4th ed.). Fort Worth, TX: HBJ College Publishers.

Reigeluth, C. M. (1999). The elaboration theory: Guidance for scope and sequence decisions. In *Instructional design theories and models, volume II: A new paradigm of instructional theory*. Mahwah, NJ: Lawrence Erlbaum Associates.

Wu, A. (2003). Theories for instructional system design: A critical review. In C. Crawford et al. (Eds.), *Proceedings of society for information technology and teacher education international conference 2003* (pp. 811–816). Chesapeake, VA: AACE.

Chapter 4
Structures and Graphics

Random Design

With a random design (Fig. 4.1), learners have complete control over their navigation of the website pages and can move through the environment in any sequence that they wish. If the instruction to be given is of a highly self-directed nature, this navigation design is a good strategy and quite necessary. An example of this type of site and associated structure is a learning environment that teaches a learner how to set up a fully connected communication network. A fully connected network is one in which all points can access each other directly. Imagine a five pointed star with lines connecting the points so that for each point there are lines connecting that point to all other points. Each page of the environment has information about a specific point along with information about its relationship with the other points. Therefore, a learner needs to have the ability to move to any point directly from any other point. When using random design, it is important that navigation elements such as return to main page, back, and so on be included and emphasized so that learners do not get lost in the website (Davidson-Shivers & Rasmussen, 2018).

Structured Designs

Learning environments without a random design have a degree of structure within their navigation structure. This type of environment has two subtypes: linear and hierarchical.

J. Frantiska Jr., *Interface Development for Learning Environments*,
SpringerBriefs in Educational Communications and Technology,
https://doi.org/10.1007/978-3-030-14482-1_4

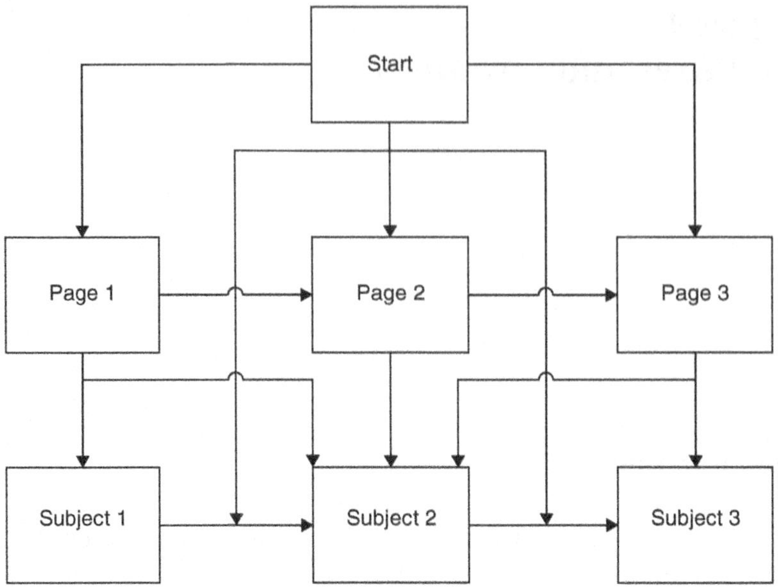

Fig. 4.1 A hypermedia-based learning environment with a random design

Linear Design

A linear design (Fig. 4.2) requires that learners must navigate through the learning environment's instruction in a precise sequential order accessing Web pages one at a time before advancing to the next. Imagine walking down a hallway with one-way traffic that has no intersecting hallways but does have rooms branching off it. Beginning at the start of the hallway, each room can be visited one at a time until the end of the hallway is reached and exited. This is diametrically opposed to the random design as there is virtually no learner control. A linear design is appropriate when the instruction requires a strict step-by-step performance or when an established process or procedure is followed. This is probably the most used design as there are many types of instruction which require strict traversal of the environment. It would apply to teaching someone how to cook according to a recipe, build a boat, learn mathematics, etc. Also, as we will see with the next type of design, linear paths of instruction can be within a larger overall structure.

Hierarchical Design

The hierarchical design format (Fig. 4.3) allows learners to begin with an introductory page and then unlike the linear design, the learner can then branch off to several paths. They are then required to progress through that path linearly and completely

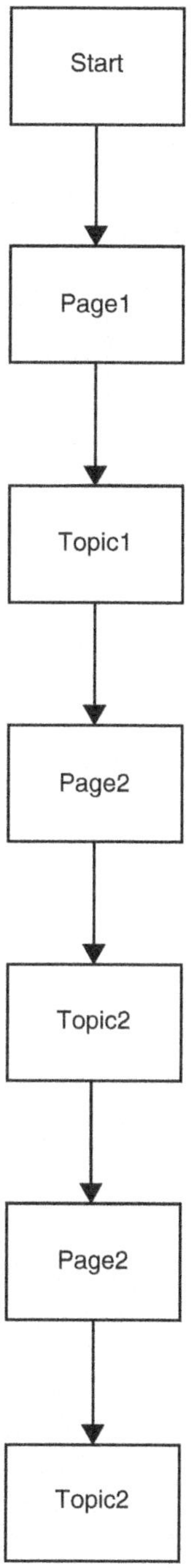

Fig. 4.2 A hypermedia-based learning environment with a linear design

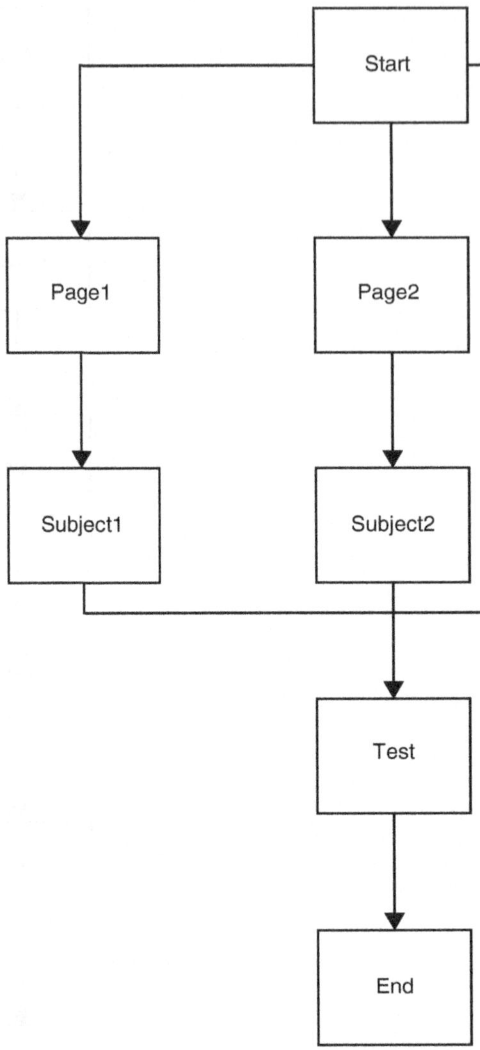

Fig. 4.3 A hypermedia-based learning environment with a hierarchical design

before moving to the end of the environment as they cannot return to the beginning of the environment. Using the hallway analogy, the initial hallway has other hallways (all have one-way traffic) branching off it as one might see in a museum with sections devoted to various eras of history. This design path can be used to move learners from simple to complex concepts. An example information domain might be automotive repair with one path concerned with transmission repair, another with electrical system repair, the next with engine repair, and so on. Due to its unidirectional nature, learners must then return to the introduction page to go to the next concept, or Web page. This design is appropriate for environments with ideas, concepts, or topics that are related to each other but not dependent on an explicit ordering of the major concepts or sections. Other appropriate information domains could be those that describe or build a family tree, teach the UNIX computer operating system, or describe the system of biological classification (species, etc.). These structures are hierarchical in nature and freely lend themselves to this design (Davidson-Shivers & Rasmussen, 2018).

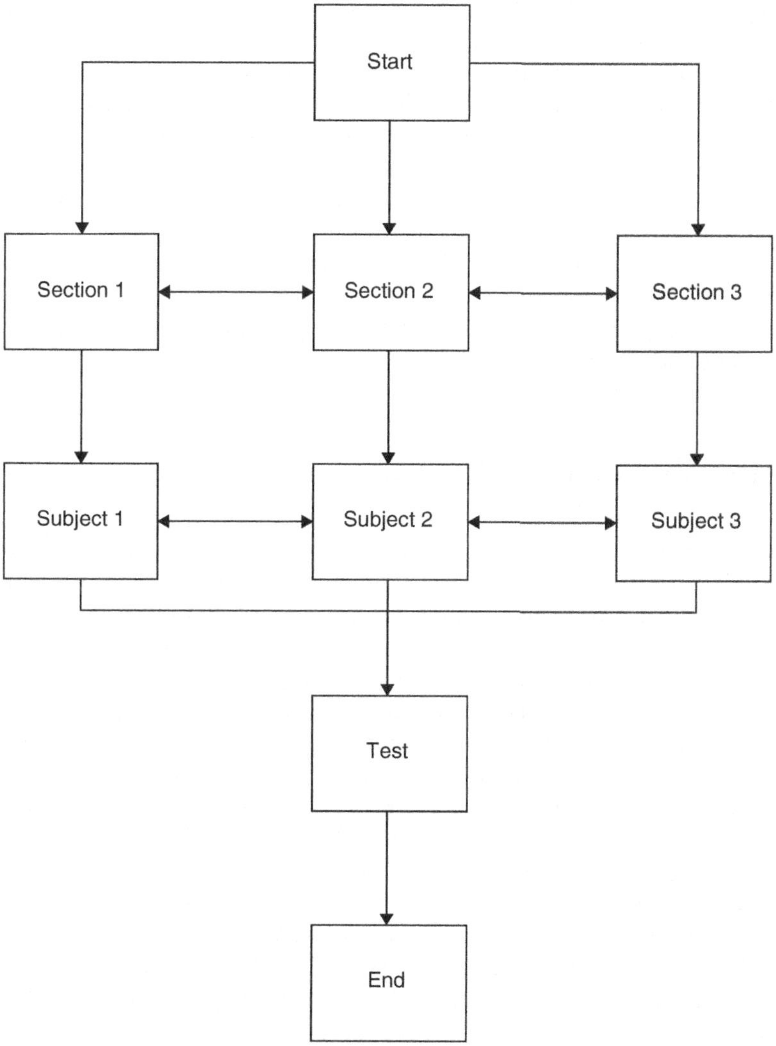

Fig. 4.4 A hypermedia-based learning environment with a hierarchical with association design

Hierarchical with Association Design

The hierarchical with association design allows learners to view an introduction and then move to any main topic of their choosing. Learners can move between topics or pages and then continue to subtopics. In the examples shown in Fig. 4.4, the section and subject pages are linked to each other as well as to the instructional pages. That is, the hallways between sections and topics pages are bidirectional. Learners do not return to the main page to go to other topics. Notice that this design allows the learner to visit the section or topic pages, but the learner still traverses the overall environment linearly prior to and after accessing the bidirectional pages. This design is good for subjects that are related to one another but can also be viewed separately.

For example, if an American history museum allows the learner to enter the museum and view some introductory information in the first room. Then based on their own interests, the learners could enter any onc of the multiple hallways devoted to various aspects of American history (technology, politics, sports, etc.) all of which are linear (one-way traffic) and arranged by century so that the learner travels through time as they walk down the hallway. Since the intersection or topic hallways are connected bidirectionally, learners can move across disciplines in the same time period; "Hmm, we're in early twentieth century technology [aviation: the Wright brothers], let's see what is going on in politics" [the Elkins Act imposed fines on railroad rebates].

Selecting an Appropriate Design

When determining which approach to use in an environment's navigational design, the designer must evaluate both the needs and skills of the learners and the type of content. There is no one best navigational structure and designers should carefully consider the implications of each navigational choice that is made.

Numerous problems can arise if an inappropriate design is chosen or the design is incorrectly developed. Sano (1996) relates what can happen when environments neglect the most important aspect of their development, the learner; "Unfortunately, many web sites today appear as if they were hurried onto the net, disregarding user's needs, requirements, and preferences." The complexity of an environment can go out of control when driven by this neglect when the designer has an undisciplined or uninformed approach without the content and learner in mind. As Sano (1996) states, "An overall lack of planning, coupled with a new-found fascination for hypertext linking, usually results in a tangled mess of web pages, contributing to users being hopelessly lost in hyperspace." Users lose their way in their navigation in a hypertext system when they are unable to act appropriately for the screen they are viewing or can't locate information that they know is somewhere in the system (Allison & Hammond, 1989; Nielsen, 1990). Overusing hypertext links, or poorly organizing hypertext links, presents a user with too many confusing choices (Jonassen & Grabowski, 1993).

Users can easily get lost while navigating websites precisely because of the ability to traverse in a nonlinear sequence through information. Inexperienced users may be especially susceptible to the confusion when navigating a hypertext site. A poorly designed and unstructured website could disorient the user. Web designs with poor hypertext navigation structures hinder usability by requiring a user to traverse too many links for needed information (Gray, 1990).

However, a properly designed and structured website allows users to quickly orient themselves and find the information that they need. Users would be able to understand the organization of the document in which they are currently positioned in relation to the initial point at which they accessed the website. The difference between a poorly designed site and a well-designed one is as clear as in a poorly designed road map versus a well-designed map (Schoon & Cafolla, 2002).

Multimedia: Its Implementation and Usage

Multimedia-based learning environments can be highly conducive to learning. Essential information and complex structures can be readily comprehended. The combination of text, audio, animation, and videos allow for eased remembering. Knowledge maps visually describe what knowledge is used in a process, and how it flows around the process. Archeological places, museums, opera houses, and the human metabolism without leaving your room can be visited. Multimedia is a mixture of static and dynamic forms of media in a single interactive application. From a cognitive perspective, multimedia can also be defined as a combination of information presented to different senses (i.e., seeing, hearing) that can interact with the user (Kozma, 1994). Multimedia is widely regarded to have had an enormous impact on many facets of education and training.

There is a general assumption that the more stimulation and media is involved, the easier it is to learn that acts as the basis of these promises. Most books or presentations that possess or discuss multimedia profess that it makes learning easier and more effective since "hearing and seeing" results make for better retention or comprehension rates as compared to "hearing alone." This supposes that there exists a simple accumulation of varying effects of media upon learning (Hasebrook, 1995a). Many of these types of simplistic theories of multimedia refer to the well-known book "Audio-Visual Methods in Teaching" by Edgar Dale which was first published in 1946. Given the time period, Dale was concerned with musical records, motion pictures, etc., rather than today's high-tech multimedia applications when writing his book. Dale felt that "symbolic information," such as words and graphics, are removed from direct understanding. "Iconic information," like photographs, movies, or demonstrations, is much more intelligible. Finally, "direct information" derived from simulation, experiments, or goal-oriented experience is the best way to learn.

In many instances, computer-aided instruction employs the paradigm that a learner receives information and then is tested on their knowledge of it and if they fail, the process is repeated. There are three flaws with this treatise:

1. The only motivation is to pass the test.
2. The learner is exposed to the content without an understanding of the context or the possibility to take different point of views.
3. The paradigm emphasizes the identification and retention of concepts, rather than their appropriate use (Hasebrook, 1995a, 1995b).

Essentially, this is the classic definition of rote learning; the most basic and primitive form of gathering knowledge with minimal cognitive rigor.

How can the effectiveness of multimedia be improved over other forms of learning? Three important factors arise: interactivity, communication, and adaptability. Multimedia and hypermedia can elicit the motivation to learn about diverse subjects such as mathematics, natural sciences, or archeology. An enormous amount of information can be stored and accessed easily. Computer applications can adapt to preferences, knowledge, and abilities of single students (Hasebrook, 1995b).

Images

One picture is worth a 1000 words. This well-worn chestnut is concise and accurate. Images play a major role in the interaction of a learner and the interface. Whether in selecting a choice via a clickable image or something that is purely informational, they are the primary elements of a graphical environment. In choosing a graphic file format to use in a website, multimedia presentation, or hardcopy document, you are also selecting what kind of picture to display. However, "picture" is not the best word to use to describe this unique type of computer file in that it is not a static, stodgy representation of something as is a photograph from the family camera. This grouping of dots of varying color represents an "image"; something that captures a real-world item or scene and splashes it as a flurry of electrons across your computer screen. This image is dynamic, vibrant, and complex. It can be manipulated and changed in ways that Louis Daguerre who became the first person to permanently capture an image in the 1830s could have ever imagined (Frantiska, 2006).

Image file formats are standardized means of organizing and storing images. Image files are composed of either pixel (stands for "picture element") or vector (geometric) data that are rasterized to pixels when displayed (with few exceptions) in a vector graphic display. The pixels that compose an image are ordered as a grid (columns and rows); each pixel consists of numbers representing magnitudes of brightness and color.

There are many graphic file formats, if proprietary types are included. The PNG, JPEG, and GIF formats are most often used to display images on the Internet. These graphic formats are separated into the two main families of graphics: raster and vector. First, let's look at how these file formats can be manipulated by a process called compression.

Image File Compression

Image compression is a process that uses algorithms to decrease the size of a file. High-resolution cameras produce large image files, ranging from hundreds of kilobytes to megabytes, per the camera's resolution and the image-storage format capacity. High-resolution digital cameras record 24 megapixel (1 MP = one million pixels) images, or more, in true color. For example, an image recorded by a 24 MP camera; since each pixel uses 3 bytes to record true color (red, green, blue), the uncompressed image would occupy 72 MB of memory—a great amount of digital storage for one image, given that cameras must record and store many images to be practical. Faced with large file sizes, both within the camera and a storage disk, image file formats were developed to store such large images. An overview of the major graphic file formats follows (Frantiska, 2006).

There are two types of image file compression algorithms: lossless and lossy.

Lossless Compression

Lossless compression algorithms reduce file size without losing image quality. When image quality is valued above file size, lossless algorithms are typically chosen.

Lossy Compression

Lossy compression algorithms take advantage of the inherent limitations of the human eye and discard invisible information. Most lossy compression algorithms allow for variable quality levels (compression) and as these levels are increased, file size is reduced. At the highest compression levels, image deterioration becomes noticeable as "compression artifacting." The images below demonstrate the noticeable artifacting of lossy compression algorithms; select the thumbnail image to view the full-size version.

Raster Formats

A raster graphics or bitmap image is a data file or structure representing generally a rectangular grid of pixels, or points of color, on a computer monitor, paper, or other display device. The color of each pixel is individually defined. All modern display monitors are raster devices. The problem with raster images is that they are made up of pixels. They are, by definition, resolution dependent. Since monitors are comprised of a series of pixels, the resolution or the number of dots available will determine how detailed an image can be. For example, a display format is widescreen ultra-extended graphics array (WUXGA) which is popular on 15″ and 17″ widescreen notebook computers. The display area is 1920 pixels wide by 1200 pixels high so there are 1920 × 1200 or 2,304,000 pixels to create images with. Compare that with an older monitor whose display format is extended graphics array (XGA) which was a popular standard introduced by IBM in 1990. Its area is 1024 × 768 or 786,432 pixels to work with. Clearly, the WUXGA format will allow you to create more detailed and intricate images than will the XGA format.

Another concern with raster images is that they are not scalable. This means that as the size of the image is increased, the pixels which make up the image become increasingly visible, making the image appear ragged. This is depicted in Fig. 4.5.

Interlacing

Interlacing is a method of displaying images on older raster-scanned display devices, such as a computer terminal screen. The method breaks up an image into sequentially numbered lines. The display alternates between drawing the even-numbered lines and the odd-numbered lines of each picture. A non-interlaced raster display draws every line of a picture, or frame, in sequence from top to bottom. This takes a finite length of time, during which the image begins to decay.

GIF

GIF (graphics interchange format) is limited to an 8-bit palette, or 256 colors. This makes the GIF format suitable for storing graphics with relatively a few colors such as simple diagrams, shapes, logos, and cartoon style images. The GIF format supports animation and is still widely used to provide image animation effects. It also uses a lossless compression that is more effective when large areas have a single color, and ineffective for detailed images or dithered images.

Two versions of the GIF format exist: the original GIF87 and the enhanced GIF89. Generally, this format stores black-and-white, grayscale, or color images. It

Fig. 4.5 A raster image that has been enlarged. Notice how the pixels are visible and deform the shape

is limited to 256 colors or shades of gray. The GIF format encodes the image information using a color indexing scheme. When a GIF image is created, the software takes the raw image data, uses an algorithm to analyze the set of 256 or fewer colors that best depict the image's color content, and creates a color table that maps these colors onto integers from 0 to 25. The software compares each pixel in the image to the color table to find the closest color and then assigns that pixel the appropriate color index value. The result is a color map consisting of all the pixel color indexes (Hecht, 2003).

GIF stores images in a compressed format. Images with large, single color regions, like icons or logos, particularly benefit from being stored as GIF files. At times, photographic images will not compress efficiently under the GIF strategy since large single color regions may not exist. Large, detailed images such as artwork, photographs, and other complex images may be best reproduced in a different format.

Design Issues with GIFs

For Web graphics, it is critical to combine the greatest amount of color with the smallest available file size to reduce the bit depth as much as possible. The bit depth is the number of bits used to represent the color of a single pixel. A bit is the smallest piece of information in computer storage and can take on the value of 0 or 1. A pixel or picture element is the smallest addressable screen element—the smallest graphical unit that can be controlled. Users of a website will grow impatient if there is a long delay in downloading images. GIF images are 8 bit images (thus the maximum 256 or 2^8 colors). Images with more colors are frequently bigger than similar images that contain fewer colors. If an image has only eight colors, the GIF format will adjust so that it will need fewer bits per pixel to map each color. Therefore, if one wants to make image files small, one should use as few colors as possible, reducing the bit depth of the stored image.

When using GIF images in Web pages, it is important to use interlacing. Interlacing occurs when a graphic begins to appear at its top and fills in downward. This effect is the result of using interlaced GIFs. The GIF stores images as a sequence of one pixel high horizontal strips. The browser receives the strips one at a time starting from the top of the image. The other option is a non-interlaced GIF. Sometimes an image will appear as a rough outline and fill in slowly. Ultimately, both kinds of images take the same amount of time to download. However, from the user's perspective, interlaced GIFs appear to download faster.

Two more advantages in using GIF images are the transparency and animation options available with the GIF89 format. GIF89 lets a designer to declare one of the color indexes in an image as transparent. This feature allows an image to be blended into the page's background color without having to recolor the original image. This type of GIF is good for special effects like fading and silhouettes. Among the GIF image format's other advantages is that much information can be embedded within it. The GIF89 format has provisions for embedding multiple images in a single GIF file, responsiveness to mouse clicks, the ability to spawn images off a base image, and for text to "float" above the image (meaning that the text doesn't become part of the pixel structure of the image beneath). Two of these features give rise to the "animated gif."

JPEG

JPEG (joint photographic experts group) files are (in most cases) a lossy format; the DOS filename extension is JPG (other OS might use JPEG). Nearly every digital camera can save images in the JPEG format, which supports 8 bits per color (red, green, blue) for a 24-bit total, producing relatively small files. When not too great, the compression does not noticeably detract from the image's quality, but JPEG files suffer generational degradation when repeatedly edited and saved. Photographic images may be better stored in a lossless non-JPEG format if they will be re-edited, or if small "artifacts" (blemishes caused by the JPEG's compression algorithm) are unacceptable. The JPEG format also is used as the image compression algorithm in many Adobe PDF files.

JPEG is designed to exploit known limitations of the human eye, notably the fact that small color changes are perceived less accurately than small changes in brightness. A useful property of JPEG is that the degree of lossiness can be varied by adjusting compression parameters. This means that the image maker can trade off file size against output image quality. One can create extremely small files if one doesn't mind poorer image quality. Such compression might be a useful tool for applications such as indexing image archives. Conversely, if one is not happy with the output quality at the default compression setting, one can increase the image quality until satisfied and accept a lesser degree of compression. Finding the right combination of desired image quality and file size will take some practice and will undoubtedly vary from one image to the next (Hecht, 2003).

Design Issues with JPEGs

In most cases a Web designer's goal is to pick the lowest quality setting, or smallest file size, that decompresses into an image indistinguishable from the original. This setting will vary from one image to another and from one observer to another, but here are some rules of thumb. JPEG quality settings range from 1 to 100 with 100 being the best.

For good-quality, full-color source images, the default JPEG quality setting of 75 is very often the best choice. This setting will be found in most quality image editing programs. This setting is about the lowest you can go without expecting to see defects in a typical image. Try 75 initially; if there are defects, then increase the quality setting. If the image was less than perfect quality to begin with, you might be able to drop down to 50 without objectionable degradation. On the other hand, you might need to go to a higher quality setting to avoid further loss. This is often necessary if the image contains dithering. Except for experimental purposes, do not go above about 95; using 100 will produce a file two or three times as large as 95, but of hardly any better quality. If you want a very small file (say for preview or indexing purposes) and are prepared to tolerate large defects, a Q setting in the range of 5–10 is appropriate (Frantiska, 2006).

JPEG images are typically chosen for use in Web pages over GIF images for two reasons: to make image files smaller, and to store 24-bit-per-pixel color data (16 million colors) instead of 8-bit-per-pixel color data. GIFs are reasonably well matched to inexpensive computer displays (due to the color density). However, full-color hardware is getting cheaper all the time and is the de facto standard on most new computers and, for continuous tone pictures, JPEG-stored images look much better than GIFs on such hardware. JPEG is also more useful than GIF for exchanging images among people with widely varying display hardware, because it avoids prejudging how many colors to use.

TIFF

The TIFF (pronounced "tif" and abbreviated TIFF) stands for tagged image file format is a flexible format that normally saves 8 bits or 16 bits per color (red, green, blue) for 24-bit and 48-bit totals, respectively, using either the TIFF or TIF filenames. The TIFF's flexibility is both a blessing and a curse, because no single reader reads every type of TIFF file. TIFFs are lossy and lossless; some offer relatively good lossless compression for bi-level (black-and-white) images. Some digital cameras can save in TIFF format, using the LZW compression algorithm for lossless storage. The TIFF image format is not widely supported by Web browsers. TIFF remains widely accepted as a photograph file standard in the printing business. The TIFF can handle device-specific color spaces, such as the CMYK defined by a particular set of printing press inks. TIFF has become the de facto standard graphics format for high color depth graphics and is widely used in image manipulation applications such as Photoshop and scanning (Frantiska, 2006).

The best format for photos used in desktop publishing documents is usually TIFF. However, TIFF isn't an option with most digital cameras. Digital photos are converted to TIFF from JPEG, the most frequently used graphics format for digital photos.

TIFF supports black-and-white, gray-scaled, or color images at any size, resolution, or color depth. TIFF is one of the most widely supported file formats for storing high-resolution bit-mapped images on personal computers (PC and Mac). TIFF is best used for scanned images intended for high-resolution printed output.

TIFF format is rarely seen on the Web because it offers poor compression. However, TIFF files can store up to 24-bit images with no loss, making them better than JPEG files for archiving images when space is not critical.

RAW

RAW refers to a family of raw image formats that are options available on some digital cameras. These formats usually use a lossless or nearly lossless compression and produce file sizes much smaller than the TIFF formats of full-size processed images from the same cameras. The raw formats are not standardized or documented and differ among camera manufacturers. Many graphic programs and image editors may not accept some or all of them, and some older ones have been effectively orphaned already. Adobe's Digital Negative specification is an attempt at standardizing a raw image format to be used by cameras, or for archival storage of image data converted from proprietary raw image formats.

PNG

The PNG (Portable Network Graphics) (pronounced "ping") file format was created as the free, open-source successor to the GIF. The PNG file format supports true color (16 million colors), while the GIF supports only 256 colors. The PNG file excels when the image has large, uniformly colored areas. It is intended to provide a portable, legally unencumbered, well-compressed, well-specified standard for lossless bit-mapped image files. The lossless PNG format is best suited for editing pictures, and the lossy formats, like JPG, are best for the final distribution of photographic images, because JPG files are smaller than PNG files. Many older browsers currently do not support the PNG file format; however, with Internet Explorer 7, all contemporary Web browsers fully support the PNG format. The Adam7-interlacing allows an early preview, even when only a small percentage of the image data has been transmitted (Frantiska, 2006).

PNG is intended to be:

- Simple and portable: PNG should be widely implementable with reasonably small effort for developers.
- Interchangeable: any standard-conforming PNG decoder will read all conforming PNG files.

A PNG image can be stored in interlaced order to allow progressive display. The purpose of this feature is to allow images to "fade in" when they are being displayed on the fly. Interlacing slightly expands the file size on average, but it gives the user a meaningful display much more rapidly.

Most graphics file formats include the ability to store some textual information along with the image. But many applications need more than that: they want to be able to store several identifiable pieces of text. Use of text tells any PNG viewer that the chunk contains text that may be of interest to a human user. Thus, a person looking at the file with another viewer will still be able to see the text. Figure 4.6 depicts a PNG image.

Fig. 4.6 A PNG image of a light aircraft

BMP

The *BMP* file format (Windows bitmap) handles graphics files that are compatible with Microsoft Windows. Usually, BMP files are uncompressed and are therefore larger; the advantage is their simplicity, wide acceptance, and usage in Windows programs.

PPM, PGM, PBM, and PNM

Netpbm defines a set of graphics formats called the netpbm formats. It is a family including the portable pixmap file format (PPM), the portable graymap file format (PGM), and the portable bitmap file format (PBM). These are ASCII files that provide very basic functionality and serve as a lowest-common-denominator for converting pixmap, graymap, or bitmap files between different platforms. Several applications refer to them collectively as the PNM format (portable any map).

Vector Formats

Mathematical definitions describe vector format graphic images. The images are composed of lines with each individual line being made up of either a vast collection of points with lines interconnecting all of them or just a few control points that are connected using the so-called Bezier curves. It is this latter method that generates the best results and that is used by most drawing programs. Vector images are scalable, that is, they can be stretched but the shape will not be distorted. Unlike raster images, they are resolution independent. Because they are comprised of shapes instead of pixels, they have an appearance like a cartoon so they are inappropriate for photo-realistic images.

At some point, all vector graphics must be rasterized to be displayed on digital monitors which are raster-based. Rasterization is the process of taking a vector graphics image which is made up of shapes and converting it into a raster image which is made up of pixels or dots for output on a video display or printer or for storage in a bitmap file format.

Rasterization can be accomplished by using several commercially available software. For example, Adobe Photoshop has a rasterize command.

CGM

CGM (Computer Graphics Metafile) is a file format for two dimensional vector graphics, raster graphics, and text. CGM is a means of graphics data interchange for computer representation of two dimensional graphical information independent from any particular application, system, platform, or device. It has been adopted to some extent in the areas of technical illustration and professional design but has largely been superseded by formats such as SVG.

SVG

SVG (Scalable Vector Graphics) was created and developed by the World Wide Web Consortium (WWWC), the international standards organization for the World Wide Web. It represented the WWWC's attempt to create a flexible, scriptable, and general vector format for the Web and otherwise. The SVG format does not have a compression scheme of its own, but an SVG graphic can be compressed using a program such as gzip. Because of its usage in scripting, SVG is an important factor in Web applications: interactive Web pages that look and act like applications.

SVG supports three graphics elements—shapes, text, and raster images. The basic shapes in SVG are rectangles, circles, ellipses, lines, polylines (connecting straight line segments forming open shapes), and polygons. YSVG graphics can be manipulated without loss of image quality.

Also, SVG is more accessible than other graphics formats for people with disabilities such as reduced vision. They can obtain value from SVG with the aid of special equipment like text-to-speech or text-to-Braille conversion applications.

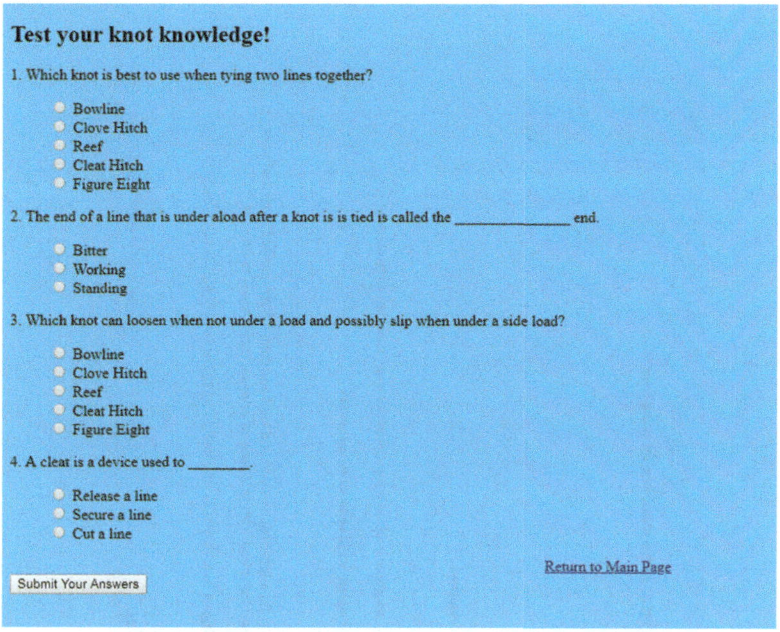

Fig. 4.7 The knot tying test page

Example Application

Due to its educational nature, the example site will use jpg, gif, and png formats. To avoid invoking rote learning, the knot tying website will employ a test to assess the learner's knowledge but only one chance will be given to take the test. Figure 4.7 shows the test page.

In order to aid the learner to address the rather arcane terminology used in knot tying, Fig. 4.8 shows the glossary page which is accessible from the main page.

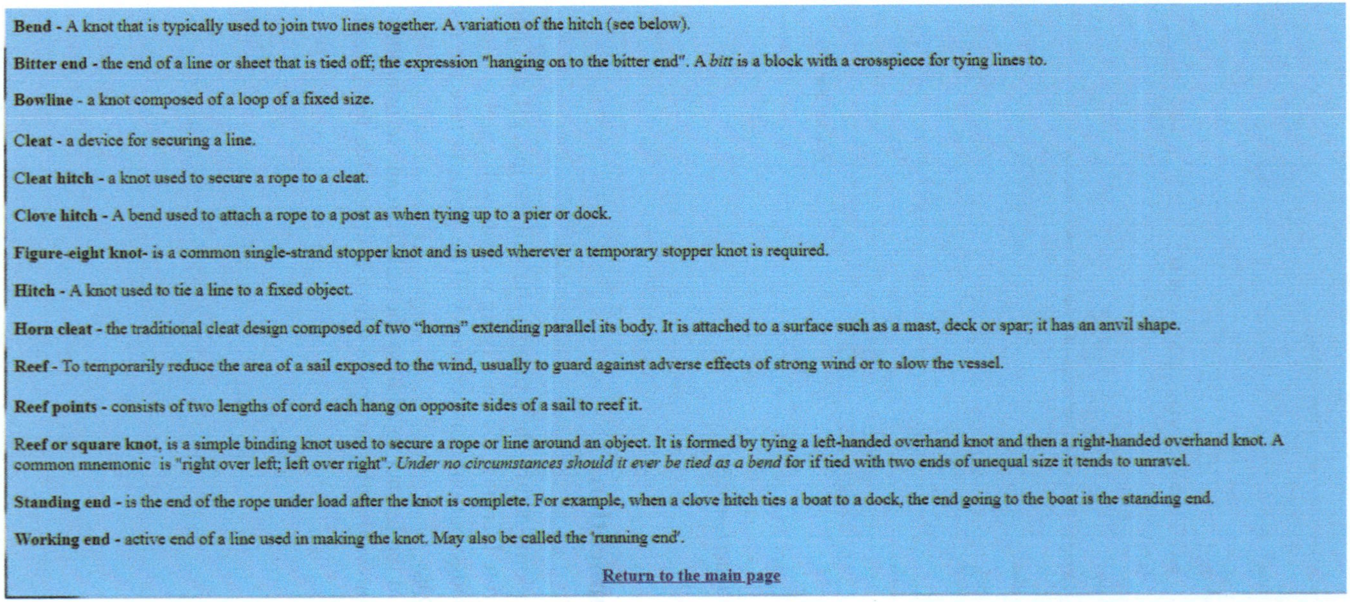

Bend - A knot that is typically used to join two lines together. A variation of the hitch (see below).

Bitter end - the end of a line or sheet that is tied off; the expression "hanging on to the bitter end". A *bitt* is a block with a crosspiece for tying lines to.

Bowline - a knot composed of a loop of a fixed size.

Cleat - a device for securing a line.

Cleat hitch - a knot used to secure a rope to a cleat.

Clove hitch - A bend used to attach a rope to a post as when tying up to a pier or dock.

Figure-eight knot- is a common single-strand stopper knot and is used wherever a temporary stopper knot is required.

Hitch - A knot used to tie a line to a fixed object.

Horn cleat - the traditional cleat design composed of two "horns" extending parallel its body. It is attached to a surface such as a mast, deck or spar; it has an anvil shape.

Reef - To temporarily reduce the area of a sail exposed to the wind, usually to guard against adverse effects of strong wind or to slow the vessel.

Reef points - consists of two lengths of cord each hang on opposite sides of a sail to reef it.

Reef or square knot, is a simple binding knot used to secure a rope or line around an object. It is formed by tying a left-handed overhand knot and then a right-handed overhand knot. A common mnemonic is "right over left; left over right". *Under no circumstances should it ever be tied as a bend* for if tied with two ends of unequal size it tends to unravel.

Standing end - is the end of the rope under load after the knot is complete. For example, when a clove hitch ties a boat to a dock, the end going to the boat is the standing end.

Working end - active end of a line used in making the knot. May also be called the 'running end'.

Return to the main page

Fig. 4.8 The knot glossary page

References

Allison, L., & Hammond, N. (1989). *A learning support environment: The hitch-hikers guide*. Norwood, NJ: Ablex.

Davidson-Shivers, A. G. V., & Rasmussen, K. L. (2018). *Web-based learning: Design, implementation, and evaluation* (2nd ed.). Upper Saddle River, NJ: Springer.

Frantiska, J. J. (2006, Fall). "Form and function: Using and understanding graphic file formats", on Cue. *The Journal of the MassCUE*, 9–10 and 33–34.

Gray, S. (1990). Using protocol analyses and drawings to study mental model construction during hypertext navigation. *International Journal of Human-Computer Interaction, 2*, 359–377.

Hasebrook, J. (1995a). Lernen mit Multimedia. *Zeitschrift fuaedagogische Psychologie, 9*(2), 95–103.

Hasebrook, J. (1995b). *Multimedia-Psychologie. Eine neue Perspektive menschlicher Kommunikation*. Heidelberg, Germany: Spektrum.

Hecht, J. (2003). File types, formats, compression and other options: Understanding and optimizing graphics, audio and video. In D. Lassner & C. McNaught (Eds.), *Proceedings of world conference on educational multimedia, hypermedia and telecommunications 2003* (pp. 1019–1021). Chesapeake, VA: AACE.

Jonassen, D., & Grabowski, B. L. (1993). *Handbook of individual differences: Learning & Instruction*. Hillsdale, NJ: Lawrence Erlbaum Associates.

Kozma, R. (1994). Will media influence learning? Refraining the debate. *Educational Technology, Research and Development, 42*(2), 7–19.

Nielsen, J. (1990). *Hypertext and hypermedia*. Boston, MA: Academic.

Sano, D. (1996). *Designing large-scale web sites: A visual design methodology*. New York, NY: Wiley Computer.

Schoon, P., & Cafolla, R. (2002). World wide web hypertext linkage patterns. *Journal of Educational Multimedia and Hypermedia, 11*(2), 117–139.

Chapter 5
Motion and Sound

Video/Animation

Over the years, a trio of camps has arisen as to the utility of animations in learning dynamic and/or ill-structured information domains. They are those that feel that the results are largely positive (Kaiser, Proffitt, Whelan, & Hecht, 1992; Rieber, 1991), negative (Rieber, 1990; Schnotz, Böckheler, & Grzondziel, 1999), and neutral (Pane, Corbett, & John, 1996; Price, 2002). Animation research covers a wide range of aspects, for instance, measurement of results, subject populations, presentation types, and study environments (Price, 2002).

Richard Mayer is one of the foremost cognitive theorists of animations in learning (e.g., Mayer & Anderson, 1992). His theory has three essential psychological expectations: (1) there exist two separate channels for processing visual and verbal representations; (2) each channel actively processes a limited amount of information at any one time; and (3) significant learning results from learners manipulating new material with old to actively construct their own knowledge. As a result, Mayer's theory predicts that narrated animations are a very effective form of a representation since they allow complex information to be presented in ways that take maximum advantage of the limited-capacity channels. He has named this the multimedia principle "That students learn more deeply from animation and narration than from narration alone" and has confirmed this in numerous studies. For example, a classic study showed inexperienced college students an animation about the operation of a bicycle tire pump (Mayer & Anderson, 1991). The students who had been presented with animation and simultaneous narration did better on post-tests than those who had heard narration without an animation (Ainsworth, 2008).

Animations aren't always successful from a cognitivist's viewpoint. Even though animations may make dynamic processes unambiguous, interpreting them is fraught with problems that dilute this effect (Price, 2002). Tversky, Morrison, and Betrancourt (2002) call this the *Apprehension Principle*: the structure and content

J. Frantiska Jr., *Interface Development for Learning Environments*,
SpringerBriefs in Educational Communications and Technology,
https://doi.org/10.1007/978-3-030-14482-1_5

of the external representation should be readily and accurately perceived and comprehended. A violation of this principle may be that the animation is too intricate or too fast to be accurately perceived (even at a lower frame rate) and, unlike static graphics, they cannot be reviewed at the learner's own pace.

Animations present information quickly; therefore, pertinent preceding states must be held in memory if they are to be integrated with new knowledge. Animations will therefore often overwhelm the limited capacity of working memory which is a temporary form of memory. On the contrary, static media such as pictures are unchanging and can be reviewed at will and will reduce the amount of information required to be held in working memory.

Cognitive load theory (e.g., Sweller, Van Merriënboer, & Paas, 1998) pays particular interest to how memory resources are used in learning has been applied to research on animations. Animations are considered in terms of three categories of cognitive load:

Animations are liable to create conditions of high extraneous load since they are not only short-lived in nature, but they may also present a lot of information in that short period of time. High extraneous load can in turn impede learning since enough working-memory capacity is not available and germane cognitive load will be exerted.

Experimental evidence for this hypothesis is gathered from studies that have attempted to reduce extraneous load to improve learning. For instance, breaking apart animations into relevant segments, allowing greater learners control in terms of frame rate, etc., and directing learners' attention to important animation elements can decrease extraneous load (e.g., Ayres & Paas, 2007). Numerous problems with animations are that they can be overwhelming as the learner's cognitive system cannot process all information effectively (Lowe, 2003).

According to Lowe, animations can at times be underwhelming if learners are inadequately interested so that the available information is not actively processed. Animations that provide a depiction of a dynamic system may present some learners with such a seamless continuity of information that they may "see the forest but not the trees." Learners may not be required to perform an intensive cognitive processing that a static depiction would. Given the emphasis within cognitive theories on constructivism, the benefits of making animations of dynamic systems too direct may be suspect. Empirical support for this prediction is found in the studies conducted by Schnotz and Rasch (2005). Learners were given animations of the earth as it rotated through specific time zones and they were asked questions such as "Why did Magellan's crew believe, upon their arrival after circumnavigating the globe, that it was Wednesday when it was actually already Thursday?" Low-knowledge learners' performance was better on these questions when they had been given pictures rather than animations. The researchers suggest that this was because learners did not perform the necessary cognitive processes for themselves and relied on the external support that the animation provided (Ainsworth, 2008).

Sound Files

An audio file format is a format for storing audio data (sound) on a computer system or media. There are numerous file formats for storing audio files. They can be either uncompressed or compressed (to reduce the file size).

Uncompressed Format

One uncompressed audio format is pulse-code modulation (PCM). PCM has been used in digital telephone systems as well as in digital audio and video for computers.

An uncompressed format would require less processing than a compressed one for the same time recorded, but it would also be less efficient in terms of space used.

Suppose that you have a file which contains a minute of a symphonic orchestra followed by a minute of silence. If the sound were stored in an uncompressed format, the same amount of data would be used for each half. If data were encoded with true audio (TTA) which is a free compression methodology, the first minute would be a bit smaller than in the uncompressed file, and the silent half would take almost no disk space at all. However, recording in the TTA format would require more processing than the uncompressed format. Everything is a trade-off (Frantiska, 2008).

Compressed Formats

Audio compression is a form of data compression for audio files that are designed to compress or reduce their size. To achieve the compression effect, either "lossless" or "lossy" methods can be used much like what was shown with graphic file formats.

Lossy Compression

Lossy compression is a method that when the file is decompressed, the data retrieved may be different from the original but is close enough to be usable. It is directly analogous to compression of images. Lossy compression achieves far greater compression but somewhat reduced quality than lossless compression by simplifying the complexities of the data. For example, you can fit more songs on your iPod using lossy than using lossless compression; and a DVD might hold several audio tracks using lossy compression in the space needed for one lossless audio track. This reduction in quality is called generation loss.

Lossless Compression

Lossless compression is a class of data compression methods that allows the exact original data to be reconstructed from the compressed data. This contrasts with lossy data compression, which does not allow the exact original data to be reconstructed from the compressed data. Therefore, lossless compression does not suffer from generation loss. Lossless data compression is used in many applications such as in the popular ZIP file format.

There are numerous areas in the K-12 curriculum where sound files can be utilized. In zoology, the sounds of animals from different species can be compared regarding their activity (fighting, courtship, etc.). In physics, the Doppler shift that occurs when a fast moving, sound emitting object races past you can be explained. The classic example is that of the changing tone of a train whistle as the train moves quickly away or toward the observer. This can be applied for most grades, while older students can be given this example as a basis for extrapolating the concept to that of light. When objects out in space are moving away from each other, their light is shifted to the red end of the spectrum much like the shift in tone of the train whistle.

Geology students can be given a new appreciation of earthquakes by listening to their sounds, while history students can be exposed to the great speeches of our time. Churchill's "Blood, Toil, Tears and Sweat" speech is much more memorable when heard than read. Language arts students can hear the many inflections of native speakers of different languages. A simple exercise in listening to the same word such as "stop" in different languages can impart a wealth of understanding to the listener. Additionally, speakers of the same language can offer the listener insight into the regional accents and dialects of the country.

Of course, the most fertile area is in music where whole symphonies or small ditties can be minutely examined for a host of qualities. There are numerous types of audio files; each has its own advantages and disadvantages depending on what you want to use it for. Some of the most popular and useful are:

Musical Instrument Digital Interface (MIDI) is an industry standard electronic communications protocol that enables electronic musical instruments, computers, and other equipment to communicate, control, and synchronize with each other. Almost all music recordings today utilize MIDI as a technology for recording music.

Waveform (WAV or WAVE) is an audio file format used mainly in Windows PCs. It is commonly used for storing uncompressed CD-quality sound files, which can be large—around 10 MB for every minute of music.

Audio Interchange File Format (AIFF) is an uncompressed audio file format standard used for storing sound data on personal computers. The format was co-developed by Apple Computer and is most commonly used on Apple Macintosh computer systems.

MPEG [Motion Picture Expert Group] Layer-3 (MP3): This format is the most popular format for downloading and storing music. By eliminating portions of the audio file that are inaudible, MP3 files are compressed (lossy) to roughly one-tenth the size of an equivalent PCM file while maintaining good audio quality.

RealAudio (RM) is a proprietary compressed (lossy) audio format developed by RealNetworks. RealAudio files were originally identified by a filename extension of

File Type (extension)	Compressed?	Compression Type or PCM?	WIN or MAC?	Advantages	Disadvantages
MIDI(.mid)	Not Applicable	Not Applicable	Both	• Wide support in many browsers with no plug-in needed. • Possible for good sound quality but depends on sound card. • Small file size.	• Instrumental only. • Cannot be recorded. Must be synthesized on a computer with special hardware and software.
waveform extension (.wav)	No	PCM	WIN	• Very good quality. • Widely supported in many browsers with no need for a plug-in. • Can record your own .wav files form a CD, tape, microphone, etc.	• Very large file sizes.
audio interchang e format (.aiff)	No	PCM	MAC	• Very good quality. • Widely supported in many browsers with no need for a plug-in. • Can record your own .aif files form a CD, tape, microphone, etc.	• Very large file sizes.
MPEG-3 motion picture expert group layer 3 (.MP3)	Yes	Lossy	Both	• Compressed so small file sizes. • Very good quality on par with a CD. • Ability to stream the file so audience does not need to wait for entire file to download to hear it.	• Larger size than RealAudio file, long time to download a song over phone line connection. • Helper app or plug-in needed to hear the sounds.
real audio (.ra, .ram)	Yes	Lossy	WIN	• High degree of compression with smaller files than MP3. • Files can be streamed from web server without special software so listener can hear sound before download has finished. Whole songs can play after seconds on a phone line connection.	• Quality is poorer than MP3 files but new G2 player and encoder increase quality. • Helper app or plug-in is needed to hear the sounds under the G2 standard. Browsers to include plug-in for older version 5 player with browser downloads.
Windows Media Audio (.WMA)	Yes	Lossless	WIN	• CD tracks ripped to WMA with Windows Media Player can be optionally "protected" (DRM-restricted) so it can only be used on a specific system.	• Does not seem to live up to Microsoft's claim of quality equal to MP3.

Fig. 5.1 Audio file formats and their properties

.ra. RealNetworks also began offering a video format called RealVideo. The combination of the audio and video formats is called RealMedia and uses the file extension .rm.

Windows Media Audio (WMA) is a proprietary lossless compressed audio file format developed by Microsoft. It was initially intended to be a competitor to the MP3 format, though in terms of popularity of WMA files versus MP3 files, this never occurred.

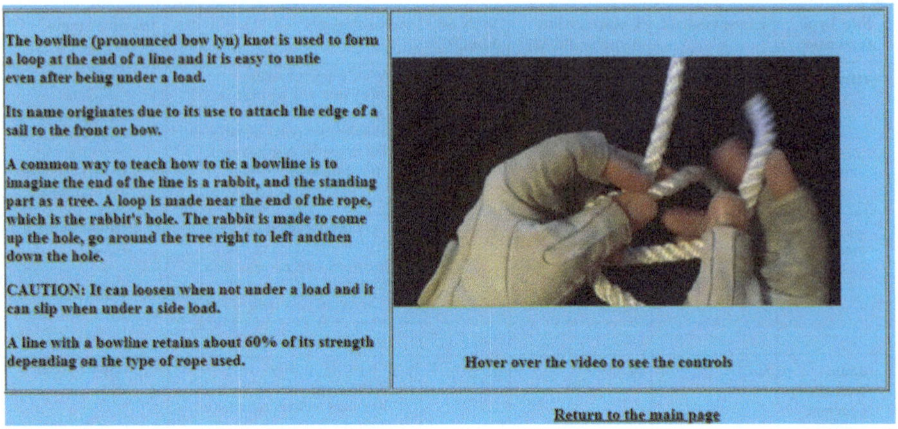

Fig. 5.2 The bowline knot video page

The WMA file format offers exclusively the ability for the files to use DRM (Digital Rights Management) encoding. DRM refers to any of several technologies used by publishers or copyright owners to control access to and usage of digital data or hardware. The various types of sound file formats are described in Fig. 5.1.

Example Application

Videos will be used to show the tying of knots to highlight the overall process as well as the salient points, while audio will be used for the narrations as applicable. Figure 5.2 shows the video page that demonstrates how to tie the bowline knot.

References

Ainsworth, S. (2008). How do animations influence learning? In D. H. Robinson & G. Schraw (Eds.), *Recent innovations in educational technology that facilitate student learning* (pp. 37–67). Charlotte, NC: Information Age Publishing.

Ayres, P., & Paas, F. (2007). Making instructional animations more effective: A cognitive load approach. *Applied Cognitive Psychology, 21*, 695–700.

Frantiska, J. J. (2008). One sound is worth a thousand words: Using and understanding audio files. *The Technology Teacher, 67*(5), 23–28.

Kaiser, M., Proffitt, D., Whelan, S., & Hecht, H. (1992). Influence of animation on dynamical judgements. *Journal of Experimental Psychology: Human Perception and Performance, 18*, 669–690.

Lowe, R. K. (2003). Animation and learning: Selective processing of information in dynamic graphics. *Learning and Instruction, 13*, 157–176.

Mayer, R. E., & Anderson, R. B. (1991). Animations need narrations: An experimental test of a dual-coding hypothesis. *Journal of Educational Psychology, 83*(4), 484–490.

Mayer, R. E., & Anderson, R. B. (1992). The instructive animation: Helping students build connections between words and pictures in multimedia learning. *Journal of Educational Psychology, 84*(4), 444–452.

Pane, J. F., Corbett, A. T., & John, B. E. (1996). Assessing dynamics in computer-based instruction. In *Proceedings of ACM CHI'96 conference on human factors in computing systems, Vancouver*. New York, NY: ACM.

Price, S. J. (2002). *Diagram representation: The cognitive basis for understanding animation in education* (Technical Report CSRP 553). School of Computing and Cognitive Sciences, University of Sussex.

Rieber, L. P. (1990). Using computer animated graphics with science instruction with children. *Journal of Educational Psychology, 82*, 135–140.

Rieber, L. P. (1991). Animation, incidental learning, and continuing motivation. *Journal of Educational Psychology, 83*, 318–328.

Schnotz, W., Böckheler, J., & Grzondziel, H. (1999). Individual and co-operative learning with interactive animated pictures. *European Journal of Psychology of Education, 14*(2), 245–265.

Schnotz, W., & Rasch, T. (2005). Enabling, facilitating, and inhibiting effects of animations in multimedia learning: Why reduction of cognitive load can have negative results on learning. *Educational Technology Research and Development, 53*(3), 47.

Sweller, J., Van Merriënboer, J., & Paas, F. (1998). Cognitive architecture and instructional design. *Educational Psychology Review, 10*, 251–296.

Tversky, B., Morrison, J., & Betrancourt, M. (2002). Animation: Can it facilitate? *International Journal of Human-Computer Studies, 57*(4), 247–262.

Chapter 6
Words

Message Design

Message design involves planning for the manipulation of the physical form of the message (Seels & Richey, 1994). Message design pervades throughout learning theories. Its principles govern the application of the attention, comprehension, and retention that allow effective communication with the learner. The specific medium used and the goal of learning play large roles in its development.

Message design is evaluated as to the effectiveness of the types of media used, their layout/presentation, and how well they support the instructional message. The textual materials are reviewed in terms of clarity, instructional sequencing and organization, minimization of contradictory or confusing media, and use of elements such as grammar, idiom, and tone. Visual (animations or static images) and audio elements are examined to determine if they support and improve the instruction and help learners achieve the desired instructional goal. Graphical devices, such as icons, links, and so on, are evaluated for their relevance to the Web-based learning, navigation, and purpose (Lohr, 2003).

Some specific evaluation questions to ask are:

- Are the goals and their purpose stated clearly and concisely?
- Does the content effectively aid in the achievement of the instructional goals?
- Is the content appropriate to the subject matter in question?
- Is the content as up-to-date and relevant as possible?
- Is the environment structured effectively to provide the user with easily accessed media?
- Do the technology applications function easily and efficiently?
- Is the organization and structure of the message consistent?
- Are there asynchronous and synchronous types of activities? If so, are they effectively combined?
- Are goals relevant to learners?

J. Frantiska Jr., *Interface Development for Learning Environments*,
SpringerBriefs in Educational Communications and Technology,
https://doi.org/10.1007/978-3-030-14482-1_6

- Are the content and structure interesting and challenging?
- Have all typographical, spelling, grammar, punctuation, and coding errors been removed?
- Is the vocabulary level and tone appropriate for the content an audience?
- Are the screens uncluttered and with plenty of white space? Are the color, typeface, and emphasis used appropriately and to enhance learning?
- Do the graphic devices function properly? Are the graphics, animations, or sound clear?
- Is the navigational structure easy and efficient?
- Are the icons easy to use and clear as to their meaning?

Message design encompasses the visual features of text and graphics as well as their placement on the page. In a Web-based environment, proper use of message design allows designers to create appealing and suitable layouts for Web pages and websites, and to ensure smooth navigation within these virtual environments using buttons, icons, and hypermedia links and through text and media (e.g., audio, video, and multimedia). Ideas based on message design help designers ensure effective dialog and interchange of information between instructor and learners (Lohr, 2003; Richey, 1986; Seels & Richey, 1994).

Directions must be clear, the information must be organized so that it is easy to understand, feedback should be readily available, and navigation should be easy and straightforward (Nielsen, 2000).

The designer concentrates on the text, graphical elements, and media to make sure that any noise is reduced and that the instructional message is clear and understood (Lohr, 2003; Richey, 1986). Noise, or interference, includes unclear directions, inappropriate or irrelevant visuals or text, poor navigational metaphors, and inadequate visual elements such as poor backgrounds, unreadable font styles and sizes, and uncomplimentary color combinations.

Message design is governed by the four main principles of simplicity, balance, emphasis, and harmony (or unity).

The principle of simplicity dictates that the elements of each Web page are easy to follow or read visually, not be too tightly clustered together, and there should not be too many different test font colors, sizes, and styles. The famous principle of "KISS" ("Keep It Simple, Stupid") is largely applicable here.

The principle of balance which refers to how the text and graphics are related can be characterized in terms of a formal or an informal sense of balance. Formal balance relates to elements (text or graphics) that are symmetrically arranged, while informal balance relates to elements asymmetrically arranged. Although formal balance is easier to create, asymmetrical elements can be more interesting and can be effective in calling attention to pertinent aspects of the environment.

Emphasis is the third and final principle and it is employed to ensure that the most essential characteristic of the information is at the forefront of the site. Visual emphasis occurs through contrast in size, change in color, and cues of arrows, highlights, and so on. Although emphasis is often regarded from a visual perspective, information presented through text can be emphasized by embedding highlighting features as the bolding, underlining, and blinking; using redundancy of information, and stating that the information is important (Davidson-Shivers & Rasmussen, 2018).

Combining Sources of Information

As previously discussed in Chap. 1, the limitations on working memory can be exceeded by the phenomenon of cognitive load in its numerous forms. Cognitive load is often introduced through poor instructional design where limits on working memory are ignored (Sweller, 2005). A split-attention effect happens when the learner must divide attention between multiple sources of information within an instructional message. For example, this can be seen when a user must extract information from a physically divided group of displays. It can be potentially dangerous as in the case of an air traffic controller needing to look at different screens during a busy day of directing planes in a major airport.

This is a learning effect inherent within some poorly designed instructional materials, not just physically separate displays but also potentially confusing or contradicting information. In this type of situation, learners need to divide or "split" their attention between these materials to understand and use the materials provided. An example of this is when two or more forms of visual information compete for attention. Another example is when fighter pilots are confronted with huge amounts of information across multiple displays in their cockpit. This may induce what is known as "information overload." Fortunately, new modes of display such as heads-up display (HUD) provide pilots with one physical display on their windscreen to get their head up and out of the cockpit for purposes of seeing other aircraft and dogfight or avoid collisions. These problems can affect air traffic controllers. Suppose an animated diagram representing an aircraft contains blocks of on-screen text about other aircraft in the vicinity forces attention to be divided between two visual displays. The diagram and text both require the visual channel for entry into the learner's sensory system. In such situations, cognitive load can be reduced by applying the modality and temporal contiguity principles of multimedia learning (Mayer & Moreno, 2003) to be discussed later. To reduce the load, the text needs to be recorded as an audio commentary, which is then coordinated with the animated diagram. Visual and auditory channels can cooperate to process the information and reduce cognitive load (Elison-Bowers & Snelson, 2007).

The multimedia-based classroom's benefit lies in the ability to integrate electronic representations that take advantage of a wide range of communicative properties (Elison-Bowers & Snelson, 2007). For example, an online instructor might wish to explain the phenomenon of a sonic boom using a recording of a sonic boom that is heard a little after the plane passes by. This can be described via text alone, but the instructional message can communicate the idea more useful by integrating audio and animation. Through audio, learners can hear the sonic boom in the recording. The addition of an animated plane that is synchronized with the sound can show what is happening with the sound waves at the point that the plane breaks the sound barrier. In this way students simultaneously see the diagram while listening to the corresponding noise during the sonic boom.

The sheer volume of information is not the only source of excessive cognitive load. The complexity of the presented information is another aspect that may cause cognitive overload. In recent years, it has become popular to give learners minimal direction while immersing them in discovery, inquiry, problem based, and experiential forms of instruction. The attractiveness of minimally directed instruction seems to center in the possibility of rich learning experiences encountered when engaging in authentic problems and processes. This approach seems engaging and may be valuable in some cases. However, minimally directed instruction has been called into question as there is little evidence for its effectiveness (Kirschner, Sweller, & Clark, 2006).

Most research on the grouping of text and sound in the recent past has examined where the audio and text are identical, and both are presented simultaneously, three studies (Barron & Atkins, 1994; Barron & Kysilka, 1993; Koroghlanian & Sullivan, 2000) have included text density as a treatment variable. No difference in the learner's attainment of the educational goal between treatments with full text-no audio and lean text-full audio was found. Each study incorporated graphics to aid in explaining concepts and ideas. Reducing the amount of text on a screen leaves more area available for graphics and labeled illustrations, which can help ("a picture is worth a thousand words") in teaching certain types of concepts.

The combination of graphics, text, and audio is rather rare in the field of research. Numerous studies have examined conventional textbook design where the text refers to a separate illustration versus an integrated textbook design with text and illustration closely grouped together. Most of these studies have indicated that physically including the text in the illustration and labeling the illustrations improved learning (Klein & Koroghlanian, 2004). This is also applicable for the design and development of hypermedia-based learning environments.

The text and illustration proximity effect is a primary example of the split-attention effect. It is proposed that the psychological effort needed to combine distant information sources reduces cognitive resources available for learning and in turn impacts the limiting of working memory. An obvious remedy for this situation is to physically integrate the information sources and thereby reduce the mental integration effort and free some cognitive resources (Chandler & Sweller, 1992). In distributing the information between the verbal and visual channels, the burden on working memory for any one channel is lower; this expansion of working memory is an intrinsic tenant of cognitive load theory (Mousavi, Low, & Sweller, 1995; Tindall-Ford, Chandler, & Sweller, 1997).

This is especially true for math, science, and technology content where illustrations are heavily used for instructional purposes (Hegarty & Just, 1989; Mayer, 1994).

Historically, studies that have examined the usage of graphics and text have used printed media. However, these research results are also pertinent to multimedia/hypermedia and can aid in the design of instruction in that medium. Multimedia/

hypermedia allows additional features of illustrations to be used for instruction, such as pop-up labels and explanations as well as animations.

Evolving from research regarding the effective integration of text with illustrations, audio combined with animation is a comparatively new field of research. Results of animation and audio narration studies have found that concurrent audio narration and animation have greater effectiveness than either alone or non-concurrent treatments (i.e., audio narration followed by animation or vice versa) (Mayer & Anderson, 1991, 1992; Mayer & Sims, 1994), while another found no difference in achievement (Childress, 1995).

The effectiveness of animation combined with audio is varied and depends upon the purpose of the animation, type of learning measured, and learner characteristics. Spatial ability and the effectiveness of animation are joined by a strong link in that learners with higher spatial ability tend to benefit more from animation with audio narration than do lower spatial ability learners (Mayer & Sims, 1994).

Historically, the linkage between spatial ability's function in a learners' analysis and understanding of animations and static illustrations is vague. Some studies have investigated spatial ability in combination with animated or static illustrations. While a few of these studies found animation to be valuable to learners with low spatial ability (Blake, 1977; Hays, 1996), others have found animation more beneficial to high spatial ability learners (Hegarty & Sims, 1994; Hegarty & Steinhoff, 1997; Mayer & Sims, 1994).

In their study, Mayer and Sims (1994) looked at animation, audio, and spatial ability. There was no analysis of static illustrations but what was examined was the synchronization of sound with animation and measured problem solving achievement for high and low spatial ability adult subjects. They found that high spatial ability participants had greater achievement measured by transfer/problem-solving items than low spatial ability participants. Transfer is the ability to use what was learned to solve new problems, answer new questions, or facilitate learning new subject matter (Mayer & Wittrock, 2006). They explained their findings in terms of dual-coding theory in that constructing a visual depiction came easier to high spatial ability learners and they proceeded to use more cognitive resources in building references. Low spatial ability learners spent more time and effort building the visual representation leaving fewer cognitive resources available for building referential connections (Mayer & Sims, 1994). Because they did not include a static illustration, there is no way to add this into the comparison and decide whether animation offset low spatial ability. The research on sound file usage with illustrations and animations may be generally summarized into four points (Klein & Koroghlanian, 2004).

1. Audio research has not indicated an increase in achievement for redundant audio-text versus text-only instruction. The number of studies is small, but there exists research that suggests text can be shifted from the visual to the audio channel without decreasing achievement.

2. There also is little in the way of audio-illustration research. What does exist suggests that moving text from the screen to the audio channel improves learning if combining the text and illustration aids understanding.
3. Research in audio-animation integration is conflicting. The existing research suggests that the effectiveness of audio-animation in instruction may depend on the function of the animation, the type of learning measured, and the characteristics of the learners.
4. Interpretation and understanding of motion from diagrams and illustrations of a scientific or technical nature may be related to spatial visualization. Learners of differing spatial ability may benefit from animation in different ways.

Modality Principle

With multimedia's two stimuli in the auditory and visual realms, a learner's brain must simultaneously encode both dissimilar types of information. Instead of overwhelming the learner, research has shown that remembrance of verbal information is complemented by an associated visual image. Working memory with two independent portions that work in parallel—one visual and one verbal/acoustic, allows for the simultaneous processing of both visual and auditory information (Baddeley & Hitch, 1974).

This finding of complementary processing leads to Paivio's dual-coding theory and was eventually applied to multimedia by the University of California, at Santa Barbara's Richard Mayer. Mayer has shown that learners are better able to transfer their learning given the multimodal instruction. Mayer explains the modality effect from an information-processing/cognitive load perspective.

Mayer tested the dual-coding theory with multimedia. Animation in conjunction with narration repeatedly gave learners a better degree of comprehension on transfer questions than those who learn from animation and text-based materials (i.e., visual only). These results were then later confirmed by other groups of researchers (Mayer, Moreno, Boire, & Vagge, 1999).

At first, these studies centered on cause-and-effect systems like cloud formation. Later, it was found that the modality effect could be extended to other systems, not necessarily based on cause-and-effect.

Therefore, information can and should be encoded as both as visually and auditorily (narration). Cognitive load is reduced if the verbal information is encoded aurally and allows them to better manage the incoming information. Mayer has since called this the "modality effect" or the modality principle. This was one of the many principles of his "Cognitive Theory of Multimedia Learning" (Mayer, 2009).

Derived from cognitive load theory (CLT), the modality effect based on the assumption that working memory, as suggested by Baddeley (1997), has at least three components: *a central executive* (CE) and two subordinate systems, *the phonological loop* (PL) and *the visual-spatial sketchpad* (VSSP). PL oversees processing verbal information, while VSSP is responsible for processing visual and spatial (i.e., nonverbal) information. According to CLT, presenting texts in audio form together with images increases effective working-memory capacity since both aural and visual channels are used to process information. Initially, this seems to be possible but when considering Baddeley's working-memory model, the modality effect does produce some controversy (Guan, 2003).

In Baddeley's model (Baddeley, 2000), CE (or episodic buffer) is a capacity-limited system that is responsible for focusing attention on the environment, and supervises and coordinates both the VSSP and PL. It controls the integration of information from PL and VSSP. Thus, working memory can be overloaded if the amount of information to be coordinated or integrated at the same time overstresses the CE's capacity. The fallacy regarding the modality effect proposed by CLT can be clearly found in the claims by Mousavi et al. (1995). They argued that (1) dual-modality presentation (DMP) and single-modality presentation (SMP) should make equal demands on the CE when coordinating verbal and image information, and (2) "more working memory resources are available for coordination when a dual-presentation mode is used because more information is likely to be held in both auditory and visual working memory rather than in just one" (Mousavi et al., 1995, p. 332).

It may not be plausible to assume that DMP and SMP make equal demands on the CE. However, the workload imposed on the CE by the SMP might not be as significant. With SMP, the textual and the image information can only get into working memory successively because people can't read a text and images concurrently. Since visual text is largely processed by the PL instead of the VSSP, it should not be assumed that VSSP will be overloaded. With DMP, the auditory and visual information must be received and processed at the same time. Since the capacity of the CE is limited, attention must be divided among the two tasks, which often results in a tradeoff in the performance between the tasks. However, with the SMP there is no such tradeoff because the two tasks are performed successively. It follows that the increase in the amount of information held in VSSP and PL cannot really enlarge the capacity of the CE but could reduce the efficiency of the CE.

There was an interesting study conducted by Jeung, Chandler, and Sweller (1997), in which the modality effect was modified. Experiments conducted to examine under what conditions DMP is superior to SMP suggest that when a diagram along with text was visually easy to process, DMP was beneficial. On the other hand, when a diagram was intricate and required detailed visual inspection, DMP was superior only when a visual aid (flashing) was used to direct learners' visual attention. Jeung et al. concluded that "the additional memory capacity provided in mixed mode presentations would only be of use if cognitive resources were not unnecessarily devoted to extensive search to relate audio and visual information" (Jeung et al., 1997, p. 341).

The results of this study have shown a modality effect limitation. However, these results are still suspect. The result showed that DMP was no better than SMP when the diagram was very intricate. This is possibly a limit point. Given that image information alone would overburden working memory; both DMP and SMP lead to poor learning results. Under the condition that the complex diagram does not produce a limit point, DMP should be worse than SMP because DMP imposes a greater stress on the CE by forcing it to process more information concurrently. If the diagram is very simple, DMP is not automatically superior to SMP since learners don't need to perform a comprehensive inspection between text and images. Specifically, the total cognitive requirements in both conditions are relatively insignificant, so the learning performance of both conditions should be about the same.

Redundancy Principle

The redundancy principle of multimedia states that successful learning occurs when words are presented as narration rather than narration that repeats on-screen text (Mayer & Moreno, 2003; Moreno & Mayer, 2002). By eliminating the unnecessary material, additional working memory would be available for processing information.

For example, a learner views a narrated animation on tornado formation (non-redundant group) or a narrated animation along with concurrent on-screen captions that contain the same words as in the narration (redundant group).

The rationale for this phenomenon is that when learners encounter both animation and printed text, a redundancy of visual information can occur. The visual channel becomes overloaded as learners expend mental effort in trying to compare the incoming streams of printed and spoken text. This can interfere with learning.

Some limiting factors of the redundancy principle occur when the captions are shortened and placed next to the part of the graphic they describe, the spoken text and printed text are presented sequentially rather than concurrently, and when there are no graphics and the verbal segments are short. In each of these cases, extraneous processing is diminished (Mayer, 2009).

Implications for Multimedia Design Limits

How can brief narrated animations be improved? Suppose there is a multimedia database containing entries based on the principles outlined in this book. For instance, for each principle in the encyclopedia such as modality, apprehension, multimedia, etc., the computer presents a short animation depicting the main points within the principle along with concurrent narration describing the main points in the principle. Thus, the multimedia explanations consist of brief narrated animation. In this context, "brief" refers to a focus on the essential steps in the process. Narrated refers to the words presented as speech; and animations refers to the pictures being presented as an animation.

What can be done to improve on the animations that have been created to help all students understand the explanations? One seemingly helpful suggestion is to add on-screen text that corresponds to the narration. The top of Fig. 6.1 shows a selected frame from a concise narrated animation for tornado formation: as the animation

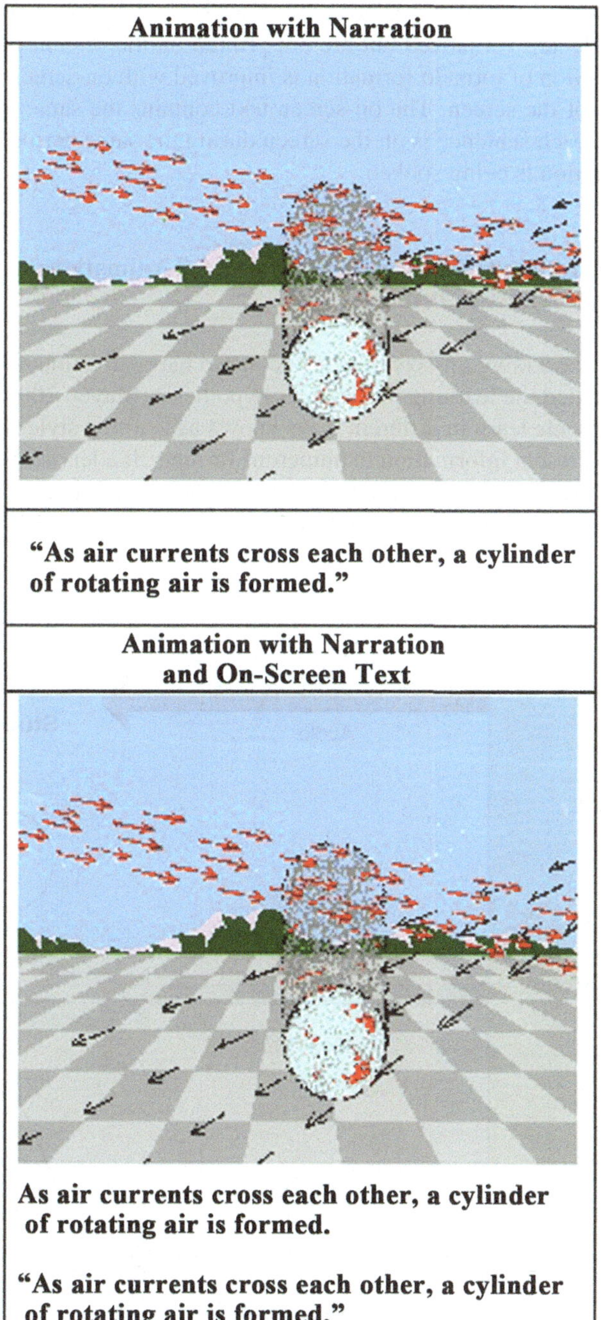

Fig. 6.1 Frame from tornado lesson with (*top*) animation and narration or with (*bottom*) animation, narration, and on-screen text

segment containing this frame appears on the screen, the spoken words shown in quotation marks are verbalized but are not printed on the screen. In this case, the narrated animation of tornado formation is improved with on-screen text presented at the bottom of the screen. The on-screen text contains the same words as in the narration, and each sentence is on the screen during the same period that the corresponding narration is being spoken.

The Case for Adding On-Screen Text to Narrated Animations: The Learning Preference Principle

The rationale for adding on-screen text to concise narrated animations is based on what can be called the learning preferences hypothesis (Mayer, 2009).

Different people learn in different ways known as learning styles or preferences, so it is best to present information in numerous formats. If a learner is more adept at learning verbally, the learner can pay attention to the narration; and if a learner prefers to learn visually, the learner can pay attention to the on-screen text. By using

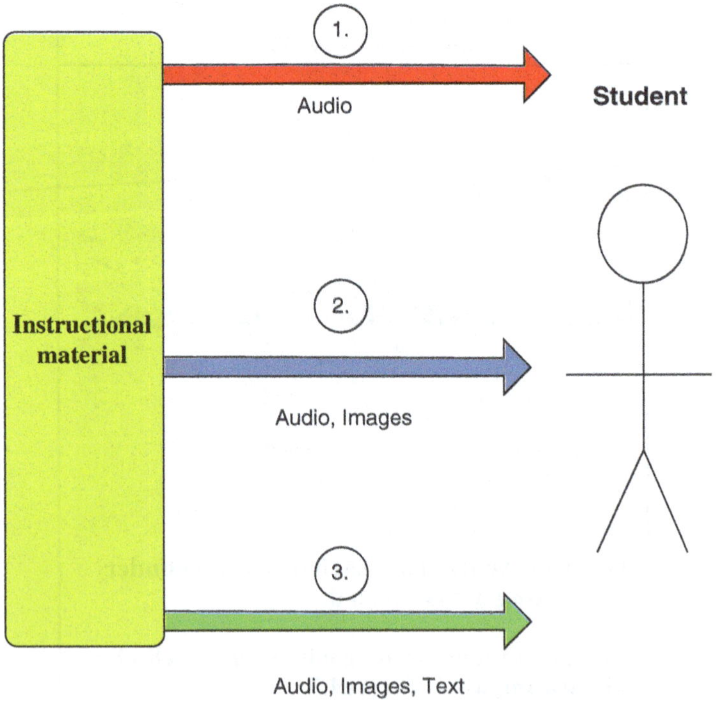

Fig. 6.2 The learning preferences hypothesis states that providing students with multiple formats of instruction and allowing them to choose the best one for their needs will maximize their learning

multiple presentation formats, instructors can accommodate each learner's preferred learning style.

The learning preferences hypothesis is shown in Fig. 6.2. The upper box shows one delivery path from the presented information to the learner, consequently just as water will have difficulty smoothly passing through a narrowed channel, the information may have difficulty getting through. Of course, this assumes that the processing is of the utmost efficiency; the path may be crowded if the learner is not efficient in processing information. If there are two paths as shown in the middle box, obviously more information can get through. Two paths also allow some information to continue through even if one path is obstructed. However, there still may be some blockage in the flow of incoming information if the learner is unable to use one of the paths. For example, the spoken word path may be blocked if the learner is not efficient in processing auditory information. If there are three paths as in the bottom box, the learner can receive more information than is available using just two paths.

Educational psychology has long recognized that there are differences in learning across individuals (Cronbach & Snow, 1977; Jonassen & Grabowski, 1993). For instance, Jonassen and Grabowski (1993, p. xii) have shown how "individual differences are learning filters." Students who prefer auditory learning will have difficulty if textual material is presented. Likewise, students who prefer textual material will have difficulty if only verbal material is presented. One solution to this problem is to adapt instruction to better fit the ways in which individual students learn:

"It is possible and desirable to adapt the nature of instruction to accommodate differences in ability, style, or preferences among individuals to improve learning outcomes" (Jonassen & Grabowski, 1993, p. 19). If specific customization of lessons is not possible, then another alternative is to provide instruction in multiple medium so that different learning styles can be accommodated. Thus, the suggestion to present words as both narration and on-screen text is a somewhat modest implementation of this general principle.

The learning preferences hypothesis is that learners should be allowed to select the method of instruction that best suits them—including the ability to choose the information format. If multiple formats are available such as images, text, and narration, then learners can focus on the format that appeals to their learning preferences. If a learner's preferred format is not available, that learner will have more difficulty in learning. Thus, it is predictable that adding on-screen text to a concise animated narration will result in improved learning as measured by tests of transfer.

The Case Against Adding On-Screen Text to Narrated Animations

However, not is all right with the learning preferences hypothesis. At the most elementary level, it is based on the information-delivery theory of multimedia learning, in which learning is viewed as transmitting information from the teacher to the learner. The reception of this information will have a greater chance of being completed as more delivery paths are available, especially when some of the paths are obstructed. This view conflicts with the cognitive theory of multimedia which dictates that meaningful learning occurs when people can attend to relevant portions of the incoming visual and auditory information and organize the material into coherent verbal and pictorial representations. They take a greater role in the construction of their cognitive processing system.

The case against adding on-screen text is based on the hypothesis that people have a limited processing capacity for visual material and audio material. This limited-capacity hypothesis is based on the cognitive theory of multimedia learning and is summarized in Fig. 6.3. When words are presented visually, an additional load is placed on the visual information-processing channel. This increased cognitive load reduces the amount of processing that remains for the animation, which also enters through the visual channel. The top box in Fig. 6.3 shows that since both the pictures and printed words are visually presented, they must enter the learner's

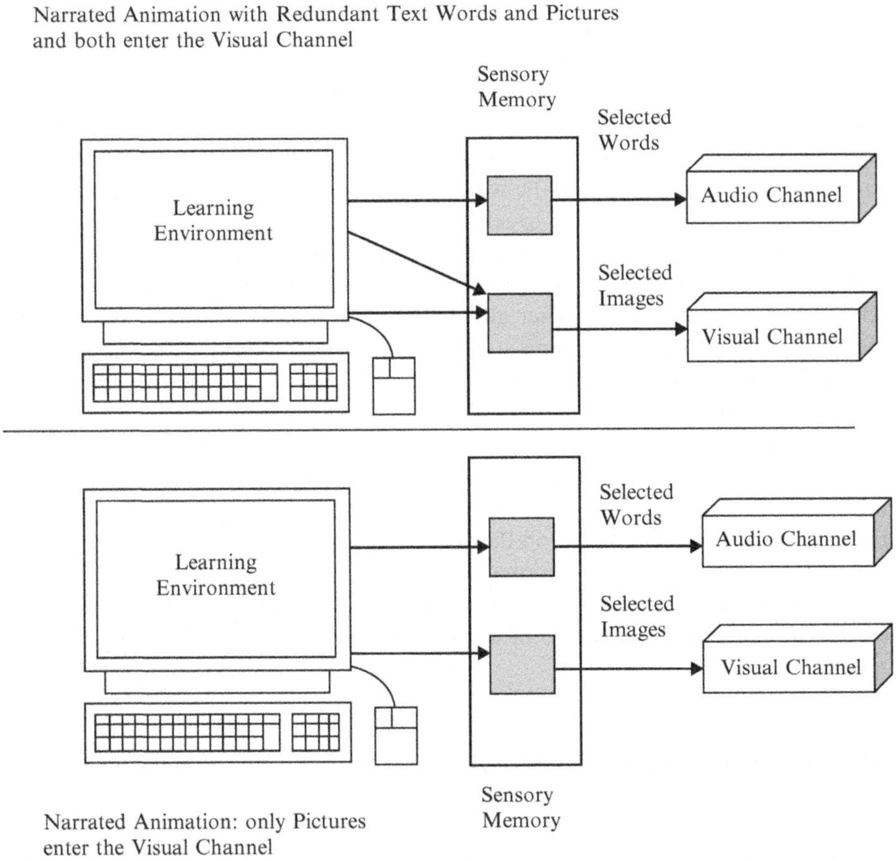

Fig. 6.3 Why the cognitive theory of multimedia learning predicts that (*top*) animation with both narration and on-screen text is worse than (*bottom*) animation with narration only

information processing through the eyes and compete for resources within the visual channel. However, the bottom frame in Fig. 6.3 shows that pictures are processed in the visual channel via the eyes, whereas spoken words are processed in the verbal channel via the ears.

When images, text, and narration are simultaneously presented, there are two ways in which the system can become overloaded by extraneous processing. First, the images and text contend for the limited cognitive resources in the visual channel since both are visually presented. When the learner is scanning between text and images, extraneous processing is created. Second, when verbal information is presented both visually and auditorily, learners may want to focus on both to reconcile the two information streams; this extraneous processing requires cognitive resources that as a result are not available for the critical processing needed for significant learning. However, the most efficient way to present verbal material is through the verbal channel—that is, as narration only—there is no competition with images for cognitive resources in the visual channel.

Miller (1956) described the limited cognitive capacity via the magical number plus or minus two. In addition to this overall limited capacity, some studies found that a limitation exists within the types of information that required processing. If two different modes (types of media) are used to present information simultaneously, learners must divide or split their attention so that they can process the information. Leahy, Chandler, and Sweller (2003) conducted a study involving 48 sixth grade students who were divided into two groups. The first group received a diagram with text. The second group received a diagram and narration. Group two outperformed group one since the group one learners had to split their attention between the diagram and the written instructions, but in group two the narration reduced the amount of information that had to be processed visually. The split-attention effect occurs when learners must split their attention between multiple sources of information, due to heavy cognitive load (Mayer et al., 1999; Sweller, Van Merriënboer, & Paas, 1998).

The split-attention effect is not without its critics. Alessi and Trollip (2001) stated, "learning is best facilitated by a combination of complementary visual and auditory information" (p. 22). Seyed, Lowe, and Sweller (1995) produced a study that successfully advocated for using multimedia since it presents information in both verbal and visual modes. Thirty eighth grade students were divided into two groups and each group was given geometry problems in two modes. Group one received the instructional material in visual mode as diagrams and in audio mode as narration. Group two received the identical material in visual mode as diagrams coupled with statements as on-screen text. The results showed the presentation of information to learners in a mixed auditory and visual mode to produce more favorable learning than in a singular mode.

Using multiple modes in multimedia instruction causes the learner to process more information since both the auditory and visual working memory must be used as dictated in the dual-channel assumption. Nonetheless, some research studies challenge this theory. Chandler and Sweller (1996) conducted a study with 30 learners in apprenticeships. The learners were divided into three groups with each given the identical task. Group one used a manual with text and diagrams along with a computer to complete the task. Group two used a computer and a manual with only diagrams. Group three used the diagram-only manual without a computer. Group three finished the task faster with greater accuracy than the other two groups. The conclusion was that the intense degree of interaction between the manual, computer screen, keyboard, and the duplicate instructions on the computer screen created cognitive load to the point of overload.

Mayer, Heiser, and Lonn (2001) also examined instructional material presenting to learners in multiple modes using two groups of college students. The first group received an animation with no on-screen text and concurrent narration. The second group received an animation along with on-screen text identical to the narration. The second group remembered less of the instructional material than the first group who saw the animation and heard the narration. The results imply that the duplication of material in on-screen text that was the same as narration was harmful to learner learning as it created extraneous processing, and this coincides with the redundancy principle of multimedia.

Other Principles

- *Spatial-Contiguity Principle*—"Students learn better when corresponding words and pictures are presented near rather than far from each other on the page or screen." (Mayer, 2009).

It has been shown that different types of information can impose an excessive amount of cognitive load. But how can the physical separation of information on the same mode affects cognitive processing? Mayer and Moreno performed a study on split-attention in 1998 and showed that learners who used concurrent narration and animations did better than those who used concurrent on-screen text and animations. A possible explanation is that learners' ability to comprehend both forms of media may be compromised by missing elements of the animation (visual) as they were reading the on-screen text (visual). After examination of ten studies about multimedia instruction effectiveness, Mayer (2009) found that there was sufficiently strong evidence for what was called a spatial-contiguity effect. They further found that learners generated a median of over 50% more creative solutions to transfer problems when verbal and visual presentations were integrated as opposed to when they were separated. Moreno and Mayer (1999) broaden these studies to include multimedia learning with animations with a study where the proximity of the on-screen text and animation was changed. One group had on-screen text that was physically close to the animation (IT group), while a second group had on-screen text physically separated from the animation (ST group). A third group used concurrent animation and narration (N group). This study interpreted the performances between the text groups (IT and ST) regarding spatial-contiguity and performance difference between the narration (N) and text groups (IT and ST) regarding modality (Moreno & Mayer, 2000).

One hundred and thirty-two college students participated in the study. The results showed that the N group scored considerably higher than the IT and ST groups in the transfer test, with the IT group scoring significantly higher than the ST group ($p < 0.001$). The findings are evidence for both a modality and a spatial-contiguity effect in transfer. Therefore, it is possible to deduce a fourth instructional design principle concerning the impact on learning of when words and pictures are presented relative to one another in time.

- *Temporal Contiguity Principle*—"Students learn better when corresponding words and pictures are presented simultaneously rather than successively" (Mayer, 2009).

With physical proximity having been examined, how might proximity over time affect learning? Significant learning is promoted when the learner can retain a visual representation in visual working memory and a corresponding verbal representation in verbal working memory simultaneously. Even though all learners receive identical animation and narration, the amount of information that they need to hold in working memory simultaneously might affect performance. If the entire animation preceded or followed by the entire narration (which we will call large bites), working memory can be overwhelmed so that it is not possible to hold all the narrative in working memory until the animation is presented (or vice versa). For example, suppose an animation is chunked with comparatively short sequences that are preceded or followed by one corresponding chunk of narration. Then if the size of the chunk does not exceed working-memory capacity, the learner should be able to make associations between the corresponding words and pictures just as when animation and narration are viewed concurrently (Moreno & Mayer, 2000).

Moreno and Mayer (1999) were unsuccessful in locating performance differences between the simultaneous and sequential narration groups. Comparable results were obtained for learning with geometry examples by simultaneous and sequential explanations (Mousavi et al., 1995). In both cases, the successive animation and narration were presented in small chunks and were unlikely to overload working memory. In another set of studies (Mayer & Anderson, 1991, 1992), where large chunks of animation and narrations were successively presented, learners in the simultaneous conditions did better than learners who were exposed to sequential presentations. To resolve the apparent contradictions, the size of the chunks that were presented sequentially to the learners was varied (Mayer et al., 1999). One group viewed a presentation with concurrent animation and narration (concurrent group), the other group either viewed the entire animation followed or preceded by the entire narration in large chunks and a third group either viewed small chunks of animation followed or preceded by small chunks of explanatory narration.

Sixty college students were used as subjects. The large chunks group scored significantly lower than the concurrent and small chunks groups in the transfer test ($p < 0.0001$). The concurrent and small chunks groups showed no difference in performance. These results allow all prior studies in temporal contiguity to be reconciled if the length of the cycles in the sequential presentations is considered. A fifth instructional design principle for multimedia learning with animations can be inferred.

- *Coherence Principle*—"Students learn better when extraneous material is excluded rather than included" (Mayer, 2009).

Previous principles show how learning can be affected by various conditions imposed on the information received by the learner. Until now the quality or relevance of the information has not been questioned. According to the cognitive theory of multimedia learning, learners process multimedia in their limited-capacity visual and audio channels. With a narrated animation, it is processed in the visual channel and the narration is processed in the auditory channel. Presenting more auditory information sets up competition with the narration for the auditory channel's limited capacity. If processing capacity is used for the music and sounds, there is less available for processing the narration. A coherent cause-and-effect sequence is created and linked it with the visual information. It can be predicted that adding interesting but irrelevant music and sounds to a multimedia presentation will harm the learners' performance. Moreno and Mayer (2000) tested this hypothesis by asking learners to view an animation about the formation of lightning either with concurrent narration (Group N), with concurrent narration and environmental sounds (Group NE), with concurrent narration and music (Group NM), or with concurrent narration, environmental sounds, and music (Group NEM).

The study was comprised of 75 subjects all of whom were college students. It found that subjects who were exposed to music scored significantly worse in the transfer test. However, subjects who were exposed to environmental sounds did not score significantly different from their counterparts who were not exposed. The relationship between music and sounds was significant ($p < 0.05$), in which Group NEM's transfer performance suffered appreciably. Group NEM had transfer scores significantly worse in additional tests than all other groups. While the transfer scores of Groups N and NE did not differ from each other, they both scored higher than Group NM. There was no significant relationship between music and environmental sounds.

This finding supports the cognitive model of multimedia learning hypothesis. Adding extraneous sounds, i.e., music, tended to harm learners' comprehension of the lightning process. Adding environmental sounds did not harm learners' understanding of the lightning process. The findings suggest that auditory overload can be created by adding non-contributory sound to make the lesson intelligible. This overload causes fewer relevant words and sounds to enter the learner's cognitive system and fewer cognitive resources can be allocated to building connections among words, images, and sounds. Thus, a sixth instructional design principle for multimedia learning with animations can be inferred.

- *Individual Differences Principle*—"Design effects are stronger for low-knowledge learners than for high-knowledge learners, and for high-spatial learners rather than for low-spatial learners" (Mayer, 2009).

Numerous theories and principles of learning have looked at individual learners and tried to determine what makes them different. Many times, his difference has been in terms of learning styles, i.e., the way in which individuals differ in *how* they learn. However, with Mayer's individual differences principle, we are looking at the degree of knowledge that a learner possesses. In this case it's not about how but how much. The term "high knowledge" not only connotes a significant amount of knowledge of a subject matter, but also an appreciable amount of prior knowledge about the subject matter. Mayer's theoretical basis for the individual differences principle relies on this as it reads:

> High-knowledge learners are able to use their prior knowledge to compensate for lack of guidance in the presentation – such as by forming appropriate mental images from words – whereas low-knowledge learners are less able to engage in useful cognitive processing when the presentation lacks guidance. High-spatial learners possess the cognitive capacity to mentally integrate visual and verbal representations from effective multimedia presentations; in contrast, low-spatial learners must devote so much cognitive capacity to holding the presented images in memory that they are less likely to have sufficient capacity left over to mentally integrate visual and verbal representations (Mayer, 2009).

To illustrate the high-knowledge learner portion of this principle, let's say that there are two pilots; John and Sally. John is an airline pilot with 10,000 h of flying experience who is certified to fly multi-engine aircraft in inclement weather. Sally is a private pilot with 200 h of flying experience who can only fly single-engine aircraft in good weather. A local flight school has a ground-based flight simulator which has an exact duplicate of a real cockpit with all controls functioning. Its purpose is to teach pilots how to fly in inclement weather. A flight instructor acts as an air traffic controller. The simulator accomplishes its purpose via a multimedia display. Specifically, the student sits in the simulator and "flies" it by looking at the instrument panel which consists of video displays of the flight and navigation instruments in addition to a video display that shows what the pilot would see through the windshield. Audio and visual alerts are made as appropriate. Throughout a simulator lesson, in addition to giving advice and instruction to the student, in his role as the controller the instructor gives the student direction as would a real controller.

When given a simulator lesson, with his high knowledge which includes a significant amount of prior knowledge, Sally will perform better at the lessons than John. Not only does Sally have more knowledge than John, he has much more prior knowledge which includes actual flight time in inclement weather. This prior knowledge will aid Sally if the simulator does not provide much guidance at times since he is experienced in actual inclement weather flying. On the other hand, John is much more dependent in the displays and voice direction as he does not know what to expect as does Sally. Mayer (2009) states that "The role of prior knowledge—that is, the domain-specific knowledge that a learner brings to the learning task—has a long and important history in research on learning." From a spatial perspective, learners with high spatial abilities can accommodate more visual information within working memory and thus can make greater use of the simulator displays and alerts.

Example Application

Principles to be used are apprehension—the structure and content of the external representation should be readily and accurately perceived and comprehended, coherence—"Students learn better when extraneous material is excluded rather than included," and temporal contiguity—"Students learn better when corresponding words and pictures are presented simultaneously rather than successively."

References

Alessi, S. M., & Trollip, S. R. (2001). *Multimedia for learning: Methods and development* (3rd ed.). Boston, MA: Allyn and Bacon.

Baddeley, A. (1997). *Human memory: Theory and practice*. Hove, UK: Psychology Press.

Baddeley, A. D. (2000). The episodic buffer: A new component of working memory? *Trends in Cognitive Sciences, 4*(11), 417.

Baddeley, A. D., & Hitch, G. (1974). Working memory. In G. H. Bower (Ed.), *The psychology of learning and motivation: Advances in research and theory* (Vol. 8, pp. 47–89). New York, NY: Academic.

Barron, A., & Atkins, D. (1994). Audio instruction in multimedia education: Is textual redundancy important? *Journal of Educational Multimedia and Hypermedia, 3*(3/4), 295–306.

Barron, A., & Kysilka, M. L. (1993). The effectiveness of digital audio in computer-based training. *Journal of Research on Computing in Education, 25*(3), 277–289.

Blake, T. (1977). Motion in instructional media: Some subject-display mode interactions. *Perceptual and Motor Skills, 44*(3), 975–985.

Chandler, P., & Sweller, J. (1992). The split-attention effect as a factor in the design of instruction. *British Journal of Educational Psychology, 62*, 233–246.

Chandler, P. A., & Sweller, J. (1996). Cognitive load while learning a computer program. *Applied Cognitive Psychology, 10*(1), 151–170.

Childress, M. D. (1995). Effects of three multimedia instructional presentation formats containing animation and narration on recall and problem solving performance (Doctoral dissertation, Virginia Polytechnic Institute and State University). *Dissertation Abstracts International, 56*, 3430.

Cronbach, L., & Snow, R. (1977). *Aptitudes and instructional methods: A handbook for research on interactions*. New York, NY: Irvington Publishers.

Davidson-Shivers, A. G. V., & Rasmussen, K. L. (2018). *Web-based learning: Design, implementation, and evaluation* (2nd ed.). Upper Saddle River, NJ: Springer.

Elison-Bowers, P., & Snelson, C. (2007). Micro-level design for multimedia enhanced online courses. *MERLOT Journal of Online Learning and Teaching, 3*(4), 383–394.

Guan, Y. (2003). Is dual-modality presentation really beneficial? In D. Lassner & C. McNaught (Eds.), *Proceedings of world conference on educational multimedia, hypermedia and telecommunications 2003* (pp. 2650–2653). Chesapeake, VA: AACE.

Hays, T. A. (1996). Spatial abilities and the effects of computer animation on short-term and long-term comprehension. *Journal of Educational Computing Research, 14*(2), 139–155.

Hegarty, M., & Just, M. A. (1989). Understanding machines from text and diagrams. In H. Mandl & J. Levin (Eds.), *Knowledge acquisition from text and pictures* (pp. 171–194). Amsterdam, The Netherlands: North-Holland.

Hegarty, M., & Sims, V. K. (1994). Individual differences in mental animation during mechanical reasoning. *Memory and Cognition, 22*(4), 411–430.

Hegarty, M., & Steinhoff, K. (1997). Individual differences in use of diagrams as external memory in mechanical reasoning. *Learning and Individual Differences, 9*(1), 19–42.

Jeung, H. J., Chandler, P., & Sweller, J. (1997). The role of visual indicators in dual sensory mode instruction. *Educational Psychology, 17*(3), 329–343.

Jonassen, D., & Grabowski, B. L. (1993). *Handbook of individual differences: Learning & Instruction*. Hillsdale, NJ: Lawrence Erlbaum Associates.

Koroghlanian, C. M., & Sullivan, H. J. (2000). Audio and text density in computer-based instruction. *Journal of Educational Computing Research, 22*, 217–230. https://doi.org/10.2190/5QVQ-3XXQ-X1JC-T2F2

Kirschner, P. A., Sweller, J., & Clark, R. E. (2006). Why minimal guidance during instruction does not work: An analysis of the failure of constructivist, discovery, problem-based, experiential, and inquiry-based teaching. *Educational Psychologist, 41*, 75–86.

Klein, J., & Koroghlanian, C. (2004). The effect of audio and animation in multimedia instruction. *Journal of Educational Multimedia and Hypermedia, 13*(1), 23–46.

Leahy, W., Chandler, P., & Sweller, J. (2003). When auditory presentations should and should not be a component of multimedia instruction. *Applied Cognitive Psychology, 17*(4), 401–418.

Lohr, L. (2003). *Creating graphics for learning and performance: Lessons in visual literacy*. Columbus, OH: Merrill Prentice Hall.

Mayer, R. E. (1994). Visual aids to knowledge construction: Building mental representations from pictures and words. In W. Schnotz & R. W. Kulhavy (Eds.), *Comprehension of graphics* (pp. 125–138). Amsterdam, The Netherlands: Elsevier.

Mayer, R. E. (2009). *Multimedia learning* (2nd ed.). New York, NY: Cambridge University Press.

Mayer, R. E., & Anderson, R. B. (1991). Animations need narrations: An experimental test of a dual-coding hypothesis. *Journal of Educational Psychology, 83*(4), 484–490.

Mayer, R. E., & Anderson, R. B. (1992). The instructive animation: Helping students build connections between words and pictures in multimedia learning. *Journal of Educational Psychology, 84*(4), 444–452.

Mayer, R. E., Heiser, J., & Lonn, S. (2001). Cognitive constraints on multimedia learning: When presenting more material results in less understanding. *Journal of Educational Psychology, 93*, 187–198.

Mayer, R. E., & Moreno, R. (2003). Nine ways to reduce cognitive load in multimedia learning. *Educational Psychologist, 38*(1), 43–52.

Mayer, R. E., Moreno, R., Boire, M., & Vagge, S. (1999). Maximizing constructivist learning from multimedia communications by minimizing cognitive load. *Journal of Educational Psychology, 91*, 638–643.

Mayer, R. E., & Sims, V. K. (1994). For whom is a picture worth a thousand words? Extensions of a dual-coding theory of multimedia learning. *Journal of Educational Psychology, 86*(3), 389–401.

Mayer, R. E., & Wittrock, M. C. (2006). Problem solving. In P. A. Alexander & P. H. Winne (Eds.), *Handbook of educational psychology* (2nd ed., pp. 287–304). Mahwah, NJ: Erlbaum.

Miller, G. A. (1956). The magical number seven, plus or minus two. *The Psychological Review, 63*, 81–97.

Moreno, R., & Mayer, R. E. (1999). Cognitive principles of multimedia learning: The role of modality and contiguity. *Journal of Educational Psychology, 91*, 358–368.

Moreno, R., & Mayer, R. E. (2000). A learner-centered approach to multimedia explanations: Deriving instructional design principles from cognitive theory. *Interactive Multimedia Journal of Computer-Enhanced Learning, 2*(2), 12–20.

Moreno, R., & Mayer, R. E. (2002). Verbal redundancy in multimedia learning: When reading helps listening. *Journal of Educational Psychology, 94*(1), 156–163.

Mousavi, S. Y., Low, R., & Sweller, J. (1995). Reducing cognitive load by mixing auditory and visual presentation modes. *Journal of Educational Psychology, 87*(2), 319–334.

Nielsen, J. (2000). *Designing web usability: The practice of simplicity*. Indianapolis, IN: New Riders Publishing.

Richey, R. C. (1986). *The theoretical and conceptual bases of instructional design*. London, UK/New York, NY: Kogan Page/Nichols Publishing.

Seels, B. B., & Richey, R. C. (1994). *Instructional technology: The definitions and domains of the field*. Washington, DC: Association for Educational Communications and Technology.

Seyed, Y., Lowe, R., & Sweller, J. (1995). Reducing cognitive load by mixing auditory and visual presentation modes. *Journal of Educational Psychology, 87*, 319–334.

Sweller, J. (2005). Implications of Cognitive Load theory for multimedia learning. In R. E. Mayer (Ed.), *The Cambridge handbook of multimedia learning*. New York, NY: Cambridge University Press.

Sweller, J., Van Merriënboer, J., & Paas, F. (1998). Cognitive architecture and instructional design. *Educational Psychology Review, 10*, 251–296.

Tindall-Ford, S., Chandler, P., & Sweller, J. (1997). When two sensory modes are better than one. *Journal of Experimental Psychology: Applied, 3*(4), 257–287.

Summary/Conclusion

This brief has shown how a systematic approach along with a set of principles and procedures can develop interfaces for learning object environments. While the learning environment is the direct recipient of this attention, the ultimate beneficiary is the learner.

As with any educational situation, understanding the audience is paramount. It will dictate to a significant degree how the environment will need to interact with them.

The myriad of procedures and concepts gives the designer a virtual toolkit. This toolkit coupled with the development approach can be employed to address many teaching and learning styles. Of course, in addition to the audience, the objectives of the learning environment will drive the inputs, processing, and outputs of the interfaces between the learner and the environment. Many questions can arise in this design and development process. What information needs to be gathered and how can they be represented to the learner? Text? Graphics? Audio? A combination? These questions can also be applied to the outputs.

The other aspect that the designer needs to address is the processing that will occur between the time that the inputs are entered and the outputs are displayed. What needs to be done to the inputs so that required outputs are created? What formats (text, graphic, audio, combination)? How do they need to be arranged so that the learner will be engaged and understand them to achieve the objectives? This is the essence of interface design and development.

J. Frantiska Jr., *Interface Development for Learning Environments*,
SpringerBriefs in Educational Communications and Technology,
https://doi.org/10.1007/978-3-030-14482-1

Index

J. Frantiska Jr., *Interface Development for Learning Environments*,
SpringerBriefs in Educational Communications and Technology,
https://doi.org/10.1007/978-3-030-14482-1

The manufacturer's authorised representative in the EU is Springer Nature Customer Service Centre GmbH, Europaplatz 3, 69115 Heidelberg, Germany. If you have any concerns regarding our products, please contact ProductSafety@springernature.com

Printed and bound by CPI Group (UK) Ltd, Croydon, CR0 4YY
05/10/2026
02228152-0005